METHOD
FOR
CHROMATIC HARMONICA

For all skill levels

by Max De Aloe

©2012 SHER MUSIC CO.
P.O. Box 445, Petaluma, CA, USA,
www.shermusic.com

For my son Federico
and for all harmonica students

Translation from Italian: Mary Riccardi
Cover and book design: Attila Nagy, zenekar@comcast.net
Cover photo: ©tonyneutri@libero.it

CD included
Recorded December 2011

MAX DE ALOE QUARTET
Max De Aloe – chromatic harmonica
Roberto Olzer – piano
Marco Mistrangelo – double bass
Nicola Stranieri - drums

www.maxdealoe.it
info@maxdealoe.it

Contents

About the Author

Max De Aloe is considered one of the most active jazz harmonicists on the European scene.

He has released ten albums as a leader and is on more than fifteen as a sideman. He has also done solo shows, soundtrack composition for theater performances and documentary films, and creative collaborations with poets, writers and directors.

He has worked with Adam Nussbaum, Kurt Rosenwinkel, Paul Wertico, John Helliwell (Supertramp), Mike Melillo, Bill Carrothers, Eliot Zigmund, Don Friedman, Garrison Fewell, Dudu Manhenga, Franco Cerri, Gianni Coscia, Dado Moroni and countless others. He has participated in various music seasons and festivals all over the world.

His professional activities are split between playing and teaching. He runs his own music school, which he founded in 1995, (Centro Espressione Musicale) in Gallarate (Milan), where he teaches modern piano, accordion and above all chromatic harmonica.

He was a teacher at the *Accademia d'Arti e Mestieri dello spettacolo* of Milan's prestigious La Scala theater.

DISCOGRAPHY AS A LEADER:
Max De Aloe - **La danza di Matisse** (Splasch Records CDH 701.2) - 1999
Max De Aloe – **Racconti Controvento** (Abeat ABJZ003) - 2001
Max De Aloe – **L'anima delle cose** (Abeat ABJZ0019) - 2003
Max De Aloe Quartetto Crocevia – **Crocevia** (Abeat ABJZ 0044) - 2006
Max De Aloe Quartet – **Lirico Incanto** (Abeat ABJZ 0060) - 2008
Max De Aloe Quartet – **Road Movie-Live at Sonvico in Jazz** (Barnum f 001) - 2009
Max De Aloe/Bill Carrothers – **Apnea** (Abeat ABJZ 0072) - 2009
Max De Aloe Quartet – **Bradipo** (Abeat ABJZ 0070) – 2010
Max De Aloe – **Un controcanto in tasca – DVD -**(Abeat ABJZ 500) - 2011
Max De Aloe – **Björk on the moon** - (Abeat Records ABJZ 105) - 2012

DISCOGRAPHY AS A SIDEMAN:
Marco Detto – **In The Air** (Splasch Records CDH 717.2)
Renato Sellani Quartet – **Il poeta** (Abeat ABJZ 001)
Mike Melillo-M.De Aloe-M. Moriconi–**E la chiamano Estate** (Philology w 188.2)
Antonio Turconi – **Lettere dal bagnasciuga** (ABLG 002)
Barbara Casini Quartet – **Uma voz para Caetano** (Philology w 232.2)
Adi Souza – **Dansa da vida -** (MAP Records LJ 30105)
Alessandro Carabelli Group – **Over and out –** (Splasch Records CDH 921.2)
Giampiero Spina - **Cinema Paradiso** (Splasch Records)
Jazz Magazine Vol.54 – **Raccolta AA.VV.** – (Emme K – JM 54)
Antonella Montrasio Mudança Quintet – **Meu silencio –** (Videoradio 000680)
Lia Invernizzi Quintet – **Nu Drop –** (Music Center BA 258)
Musica Jazz Raccolta AA.VV. - **Abeat Story –** (MJCD 1234)
Antonio Marco Turconi – **Di sole, di pioggia o di vento –** (LAB 104)
Antonella Montrasio e Max De Aloe Quartet – **Pingo Pingando –** (Abeat ABJZ 511)
Andrea Celeste – **Something Amazing –** (Zerodieci)

Introduction

This method book is the result of over twenty years of individual study of the chromatic harmonica and an equal amount of time devoted to instructing many students on harmonica playing. Much was also gained from numerous collaborations with a variety of musicians who have taught me a great deal.

After a long period of studying the piano, I stumbled on the chromatic harmonica while still very young. It was a chance encounter that was to change more than just my musical life. I have had a great love affair with the chromatic harmonica ever since, which seems stronger with every passing day, like a long, happy marriage founded on passion, complicity, amusement and joy, with moments of yielding and sacrifice too.

I believe that coming to the chromatic harmonica with a good knowledge of music in place and a fair amount of live performance experience helped me realize immediately that most existing method books for chromatic harmonica fail to put forth an in-depth study of the instrument. Most method books didn't (and still don't) make use of staves, ignoring the practice of notated music entirely. Do you know of any method books for saxophone, trumpet, piano, or any other instrument that don't make use of musical notation? Why is this typically the case with the chromatic harmonica? I have, therefore, had to put together my own teaching tool, used first on myself, then on my students, which, while similar to the methodology used for more traditional instruments, hopefully offers up a dynamic and modern perspective.

A central influence during my formative years was the help and musical expertise of a great teacher, Willi Burger, one of the world's major classical virtuosi of the chromatic harmonica. In addition, the knowledge gained through seminars taught by other musicians, mainly pianists, trumpeters and arrangers, was also key. I have always strived to work with musicians more skilled and talented than myself in order to learn from them.

In this method book the chromatic harmonica is treated as a musical instrument in all respects, and rightly so. Tablatures (certainly more useful to the diatonic harmonica), will not be used nor aperture numbers placed above notes. The study course is an accessible one, devised for everybody, but will inevitably present some challenges which will require diligence from the reader.

For example, a good soccer coach knows that the player should know the rules of the game, acquire a good overview of the playing field, have good breathing technique, athletic preparation, ball technique, know how to kick both on the left and right, with his head, stop, run, kick penalties, respect the other players, be ready to yield, be prepared to make sacrifices, but also know how to enjoy himself while playing. The same holds true for a good teacher with regard to a student wishing to learn an instrument. The study and practice of a musical instrument is manifold: it works on different levels and touches upon different subjects – music theory, solfège, harmony, instrumental technique, reading skills, rhythmic proficiency and independence, speed, developing a good sound, possible improvisational skills and much more. My aim in compiling this method book has been to devise a course of study for the student where he/she can gradually "train" various technical aspects of playing, above all as they relate to the difficulties of the chromatic harmonica, an instrument which is not as easy as it might seem. Step by step, key by key, each chapter attempts to accustom the student to having a complete overview of the instrument through exercises and tunes chosen for various purposes.

Naturally a method book cannot contain absolutely everything. In the following pages, we will often just touch on ideas that can be expanded on with the help of other method books and pieces. For example, I have intentionally omitted examining music theory and harmony as well as rhythmic, melodic and vocal solfège, but I reference texts where all these can be learned and studied in more detail.

Considering my own musical education, the pedagogy I have adopted is obviously oriented towards jazz music, although the basis of study is perfectly suited to all genres of music. Furthermore, I have avoided delving into the world of jazz improvisational technique, as this is already dealt with in highly effective method books common to all instruments. I am sure that everyone who completes this study book will have acquired a good base from which to take on any manual of improvisation techniques.

Naturally, every method cannot state "absolute truth" with respect to its subject. This book inevitably contains a conception of music and the instrument that is a reflection of myself. But I am positive that if the following suggestions are adopted step by step, much will be learned about the chromatic harmonica. My one great wish is that this book succeeds in helping whoever wishes to deepen his/her knowledge of, and passion for, a fascinating instrument, and that in the end, he/she can really draw enjoyment from it.

In conclusion, I feel I must state that beyond the study of an instrument, it is important to listen to great amounts of music with care and passion. It may seem like a banal suggestion, but I have often encountered students wishing to play jazz music who rarely listened to it. It would be like studying to become a film director without ever watching a film. Let's not limit ourselves then to only listening to harmonica players. Ours is an instrument still largely to be discovered, therefore we have much to learn from all other instrumentalists and from music in its totality. Let's widen our scope on music as much as possible, encompassing all different genres, historic periods and–above all–let's enjoy ourselves.

Good luck to everyone and enjoy your studies.

Max De Aloe

Chapter One

Chromatic Harmonica: The Basics

The harmonica is classified in the so-called "free reed" instrument family, which includes, among the most important, the accordion, bandoneon, concertina, reed organ and harmonium. The free reed is a screwed or riveted metal blade set into vibration by air pressure produced by the mouth or by bellows. The pitch of the reed is determined by its length, shape and thickness.

There are mainly two types of harmonica: the diatonic harmonica and the chromatic harmonica.

The diatonic is the most popular and is built to play in only one key, though techniques such as bending and over-bending make it possible to play the entire chromatic scale.

The chromatic harmonica is distinguished by its larger size and by a button on its right side called the slide. The chromatic harmonica can produce all notes (for the sake of simplicity: all the white and black keys on a piano) from a range of two and a half octaves (10-hole chromatic harmonica) to over four octaves (16-hole chromatic harmonica), depending on the model. Substantially, such a small instrument can produce the same or even a greater number of notes found on most other musical instruments.

This method book is intended for the 12-hole chromatic harmonica in the key of C (three octave range), since this is the instrument most harmonica players use.

The skill acquired from this method book can be easily transferred to a 10-hole chromatic harmonica (which lacks the last two holes of a three-octave-harmonica) or a 16-hole chromatic harmonica (featuring an extra octave below middle C).

Let's first understand how the notes are positioned on the harmonica.

It is important to note that some notes on the harmonica are played only by blowing and others only by drawing air. When the slide is pressed, it is possible to transpose a note one half-step higher. In the beginning, we will learn to play without operating the slide, introducing it later on in the fifth chapter, once the initial challenges of positioning are no longer an issue.

1.1 DIAGRAM OF THE NOTES ON A 12-HOLE CHROMATIC HARMONICA IN KEY OF C

BLOWN		C	E	G	C	C	E	G	C	C	E	G	C
WITHOUT SLIDE	**HOLE**	1	2	3	4	5	6	7	8	9	10	11	12
DRAWN		D	F	A	B	D	F	A	B	D	F	A	B

hole 1: C blown – D drawn (Middle C is located on the first hole)
hole 2: E blown – F drawn
hole 3: G blown – A drawn
hole 4: B drawn – C blown

From the fifth hole on, the same sequence follows one octave higher

hole 5: C blown – D drawn
hole 6: E blown – F drawn
hole 7: G blown – A drawn
hole 8: B drawn – C blown

The same applies from hole 9 to hole 12, with the exception of the 12th hole, where a high D sounds while blowing and pressing the slide

hole 9 : C blown – D drawn
hole 10: E blown – F drawn
hole 11: G blown – A drawn
hole 12: B drawn – C blown

Pressing the slide, as shown below, raises each note a half-step

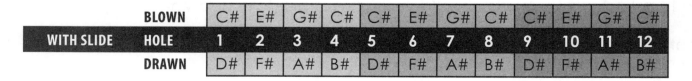

BLOWN		C#	E#	G#	C#	C#	E#	G#	C#	C#	E#	G#	C#
WITH SLIDE	**HOLE**	1	2	3	4	5	6	7	8	9	10	11	12
DRAWN		D#	F#	A#	B#	D#	F#	A#	B#	D#	F#	A#	B#

POSITIONING THE HARMONICA

The harmonica is held with the left thumb (from below), and the index finger and the middle finger (optional) from above. The thumb and two fingers are aligned along the harmonica, while the ring and little finger will serve to hold the microphone whenever amplification is needed. The right index finger activates the slide. An old instrument hold has the right index finger held vertically straight, pressing the slide with the fleshy part of the finger. However, many harmonica players play pressing the slide with other parts of the index finger below the fingertip.

The harmonica is be held parallel to an imaginary horizontal line crossing both the player's eyes, and its position shouldn't change while playing. Rather, the musician's head must move in search of the notes while the instrument remains stationary. Various effects can be made by moving the harmonica, but this will be discussed further on.

If the instrument requires amplification, a hand-held dynamic microphone suitable for vocals is very practical. The microphone is held with the ring and little finger, and possibly the middle finger, of the left hand. It will have to be slid along the harmonica in order to provide even amplification for all notes. If one moves from a note played on the first hole to one played on hole 10, the position of the microphone should change accordingly.

HOW TO PLAY THE HARMONICA

There are two existing ways to play the harmonica:

1. The Whistle Method

Perhaps the most spontaneous way, it consists of playing the instrument by closing the mouth around the embouchure as if preparing to whistle. How much the mouth closes is determined by the fact of producing just one note at a time. This is our point of reference. If we hear more than one note when blowing or drawing, then our lips are either not puckered enough on the embouchure or we are halfway between two notes. By feeling with the tip of the tongue, we can find out if we are aligned with the correct hole. When doing so, some harmonica players curl their tongue into a U-shape, channeling the air stream through the middle. This is a little-used technique, in part because not everybody's tongue is flexible enough. Of the harmonica players I have met, the great Bruno De Filippi used this technique.

2. The Tongue Blocking Method

With this method, the tip of the tongue is used to cover the hole to the left of the one selected while playing the desired note with the right side of the mouth. For example, if we wish to play a blown C through the fifth hole, we place our mouth on the fourth and fifth holes and block the airflow to the fourth hole with the tip of the tongue, letting the air stream through the right side of the mouth into the fifth hole, sounding the C.

It is difficult, if not impossible, to determine which technique is better or more spontaneous. I suggest you try them both and see which one best suits the shape of your mouth or simply feels better. There's no need to hurry in choosing, but I'd venture to say it won't be difficult to determine which feels most natural to you. There are teachers who encourage the student to learn both techniques by playing exercises in both ways. As for me, I play using the whistle technique though I made an effort, during the first two years of my studies, to perform all exercises with both techniques. However, from the very beginning I was sure I was going to use the whistle method. There are teachers and good harmonica players who favor one technique over the other or believe one suits a certain musical genre more than the other. I believe that the student should be given the freedom to approach the instrument in the most natural and spontaneous manner possible, at least as far as these two techniques are concerned. In my teaching experience I find more students are at ease with the whistle technique, but I have also seen the opposite.

Important: all exercises and advice you encounter in this method book pertain to both the Whistle Method and the Tongue Blocking Method.

BREATHING

As with all wind instruments, good breathing technique on the harmonica is essential for sound projection. The harmonica is peculiar in that it is the only wind instrument played by both blowing and drawing air. Harmonica playing requires conforming to all basic principles of diaphragmatic-thoracic breathing. The diaphragm is a muscle lamina that can be thought of as a floor separating the thoracic and the abdominal cavities.

The basic breathing technique that is the departure point for playing the harmonica is as follows: contract the diaphragm (pushing it inwards and lifting it) to blow, and relax it to inhale.

In order to easily understand the diaphragm's location inside our body, we can simulate a yawn while resting a hand on our abdomen.

Keep in mind that intercostal, thoracic and abdominal muscles also contribute to the process of inhaling and exhaling.

When playing high notes, the process of contraction and release of the diaphragm normally happens in the upper abdomen. When blowing and drawing in the high octave, the area right below the sternum is what we should feel working. With high notes--again--greater pressure and greater activity is required in the upper abdomen. With low notes, the movements of the diaphragm happen in a more relaxed way, requiring more air but less pressure. Sounding low notes acts upon the lower abdomen.

As far as posture is concerned, we must get used to playing both standing and sitting down. The head should be held upright, facing straight ahead, the chin slightly lifted. Let's avoid keeping our chin low as if watching the tips of our shoes and avoid resting the elbows against the chest, too. Each person ultimately finds a position that permits him to feel relaxed at all times. When practicing any instrument it is always important to be relaxed while playing. Back to the harmonica--the tongue generally sits low so as not to obstruct the flow of air. The tip of the tongue rests delicately on the lower front teeth.

Let's not--and this is very important--worry ourselves to the point of exasperation over these details. Instead, begin playing and trying to produce sounds; later on we can test out the results of a performance that takes into account the concepts laid out about breathing and tongue position.

It makes good sense to follow advice concerning positioning in general, but when we begin playing it is equally important that our body not be excessively focused on its posture, the tongue's position or breathing.

WHICH HARMONICA TO USE

The best-known brands of harmonica are *Hohner, Suzuki, Hering, Tombo,* and *Bends.* Even if the distribution and circulation of these brands varies depending on the country, it isn't easy to find a wide selection of models.

The German brand *Hohner,* a leader in this field, has been manufacturing harmonicas since the last century and is, objectively, the most highly distributed brand in the world.

The most played harmonica model, and the one I suggest to whoever wishes to approach the instrument, is the *Hohner Chromonica 270* (12 holes). It is an optimal instrument for both the beginner and professional, not overly expensive, though models similar to this one in both style and price exist also by other manufacturers.

Toots Thielemans used this instrument for over thirty years, later developing the *Toots* model, an evolution of the *Chromonica 270.* Two sub-models exist of the *Toots* model, both featuring 12 holes: the *Mellow Tone* (softer sounding) and the *Hard Bopper* (more reactive and aggressive).

There are also 16-hole models by *Hohner*, such as the *Chromonica 280* or the *Super 64*. The only interesting aspect of these models is the possibility of playing an extra low octave, but I think they are more cumbersome and less functional than the 12-hole. Thielemans himself rarely used this kind of harmonica during his entire career. I believe he did so only for a limited period of time during the '70s.

It could be interesting to use a 16-hole harmonica in specific compositions calling for low notes which undoubtedly have a certain appeal.

In contrast, I cannot see the purpose in using a 10-hole harmonica (*Chromonica 260*) instead of a 12-hole. Perhaps the only advantage for the beginning player is that a 10-hole costs slightly less than a 12-hole, and can serve to help someone beginning to study the instrument.

I feel compelled to repeat that there are many different brands of models available that are certainly all worth a try. But there will be plenty of time for this. The important thing is to start on a functional, standard model. One quite problematic aspect of the harmonica is that the reeds tend to wear out when played, with few ways of replacing them. Either you're lucky enough to find the extremely rare repairman, or you become an excellent technician yourself (granted that you have the spare parts needed). There's no getting around it: the reeds are destined to lose their tuning or break. I do suggest that you avoid playing on the newly bought harmonica too hard. It is important, as well, not to play with food residues still in the mouth.

A useful piece of advice is to never expose the harmonica to sudden changes of temperature. It mustn't be left in the car on very hot or very cold days, just as it mustn't be left near a heat source. Remember to warm up the harmonica in your hands before playing it so that the temperature of the instrument is similar to the temperature of your breath. Limiting this difference greatly reduces condensation/moisture problems inside the instrument.

Chapter Two

Let's play – exercises on the middle octave

Now let's play, beginning with the first exercise.

Initially we'll only play in the middle octave (second octave: from hole 5 to hole 9), since these notes are easier to produce than the lower or higher ones. On wind instruments, playing notes at the top and bottom of the range is generally more complex.

In order to play, our mouth should move along the harmonica in a sliding motion, from one hole to the next, while keeping the harmonica still.

Exercise 2.1 consists of long notes to be played trying to sustain the sound. Let's play single notes; at this stage, don't worry about connecting the notes, just strive to make them sound.

Remember what has been said about breathing. The tongue, if using the *Whistle Method*, will serve to aim, meaning we'll rest the lips on the harmonica, then using the tip of the tongue seek out the hole to blow or draw; once it feels perfectly centered, we retract the tongue to the bottom of our mouth and emit the sound. Basically, the tongue aims so that we understand if we are positioned correctly in relation to the note to be played.

If we hear two notes sounding instead of just one, the so-called "accordion effect", it means our mouth is misaligned with the hole of the selected note. Most likely, the mouth doesn't adhere well to the embouchure and some air is escaping. Or we find ourselves halfway between two notes. Using the tongue to aim, let's play it once more.

2.1

The following exercise trains us to repeatedly play two notes located in the same hole—continually alternating a blown and a drawn note.

Don't expect the notes to be perfect immediately. Some notes may be difficult to sound or you may get out of breath. Instead of worrying, simply play and replay them until they improve.

These difficulties will be overcome through lots of practice and determination and will be even more evident and annoying when we play high and low notes. While practicing these exercises, keep in mind the position of the instrument, the breathing principles and, above all, take care not to insert the instrument too far into the mouth, not to "eat it" too much.

Some notes will probably not sound so rich and full. Don't worry for the time being. Remember, it will take us time and patience.

"Try and try again" must become our motto when studying.

2.2

The first two exercises are of great importance and are useful in approaching the instrument (sounding of notes, clean execution and breathing). Exercise 2.3 adds another challenge: that of moving the mouth to an adjacent hole.

For example, when playing the first three notes, C – D are played one blown and one drawn in hole 5; we then move to hole 6 to play a blown note, only to return to hole 5 to play the drawn D. The transitions between these three notes will have to be repeated many times over: this is the meaning of the repeat sign. The exercise must be played extremely slowly. Be careful switching between the drawn D in hole 5 and the blown E in hole 6. It isn't a very natural transition, as it requires shifting the mouth. It is to be played repeatedly, as are the following passages starting on D, then E and finally F.

Attention: when moving from one hole to the next, we slide the mouth along without separating it from the embouchure. This is an important point: the mouth slides along the embouchure and does not jump in search of the note.

This exercise illustrates the difficulty, and at the same time the importance, of connecting one note to the next. We should try not to leave even the smallest space, so-called staccatos, between notes when we change holes. The harmonica player gives fluidity to his notes by imitating the fluidity of normal breathing.

2.3

Now we'll play the notes from C to A and back in a more continuous manner, remembering to blow and draw deeply. Let the notes be heard. Don't play too softly for fear of making mistakes, but don't attack the instrument with an excessive amount of air either.

2.4

Attention: before going on to new exercises, let's focus on a possible problem which may have arisen. When playing blown notes, it sometimes happens that we exhale some air through the nose at the same time. In other words, air "leaks" from the nose resulting in weaker sounding notes. What's more, apart from the diminished intensity of sound, it also reduces the control we exert on the note played. As a result, there is less volume and less control of timbre which will compromise our efforts later on to achieve the vibrato effect and compromise the correct arrangement and fluidity between blown and drawn notes. It is simple to find out if we are "leaking" air: place a finger close to the nose when sounding a blown note and feel whether air flows out of it. If so, return to playing one single blown note and focus on keeping the air flowing only through the mouth. While playing the note, hold the harmonica with only one hand; with two fingers of the other hand, close the nostrils repeatedly, and listen for any change in sound. No change in sound heard when blocking and unblocking the nostrils means you have achieved the correct way of playing.

When we get to this point, we'll play several blown notes checking for possible "air leaks." "Leaking" can be a useful technique, but only once we can control it voluntarily. For example, when a tune has many consecutive drawn notes, the first blown note can be used to "leak" a bit of air through the nose in order to restore the proper equilibrium to the breath. But let's be very careful: even when done consciously, "leaking" air from the nose will always alter our sound a bit. It should be used carefully and definitely not on the "important" notes of a tune.

The following exercise brings us something new: two consecutive drawn notes, A (hole 7) and B (hole 8), as well as playing the high C and D. Always play the high C blowing in hole 9 and avoid the C blown in holes 4 and/or 8. Personally, I rarely suggest playing the C in holes 4 and 8 blown, especially to the beginner. Instead I suggest using holes 5 and 9 blown, and of course holes 1 and 12. Back to the two consecutive drawn notes, they can be problematic to our breathing and might sound weaker compared to blown notes; but try not to get discouraged. Moving from one hole to the next with two drawn notes is tiring initially and will remain so for quite a while, but things will eventually improve.

2.5

The exercises presented up to this point should be played rigorously, seeking to produce clean-sounding notes, breathing the correct way and in a legato manner. Only after some days of practice will we be able to perform the following exercise, the ascending and descending C major scale.

The scale should be played slowly, giving each note the same duration. We'll feel short of breath, similar to what we feel when running without having trained. Let's not stop after only one or two repetitions. We need to learn to breathe with our instrument and manage the breathlessness as something surmountable. Also, don't worry if your mouth feels glued to the embouchure, unable to properly slide along the instrument. It is very normal to have problems with salivation in the beginning. Simply moisten your lips before starting to play and every now and then during breaks, quickly flick the tongue over the lips. With practice, this problem will also vanish. At any rate, I strongly advise against anchovy-pizza or pasta right before playing!!!

Apart from this dietary advice, with the suggestions explained so far we are now already able to perform many exercises on the central octave of our harmonica.

If we wish to seriously study this instrument, let's avoid immediately trying to play melodies and employing the slide; instead, let's concentrate on the key elements I've highlighted (clean notes, breathing, legato, etc.).

2.6

In playing the C major scale, we are already presented with one of the structural faults of the instrument. The scale ascending from C to high C requires the following transitions: blow – draw – blow – draw – blow – draw – draw – blow. The sequence of two draws on notes A and B breaks the cycle of breathing established over the first six notes (blow – draw – blow – draw – blow – draw). On the harmonica, scales, melodies and arpeggios can occur with many consecutive notes either all blown or all drawn. There is no real pattern, or practically none, for scales, like there is with other musical instruments. With the harmonica we are always forced to think of the notes in relation to their position. Patterns or formulas are of little use. This concept will become clearer as we carry on. This "obstacle" is also the source of the instrument's charm. An instrument that is even more complex from this point of view is the diatonic bandoneon (for clarity, the one used in the tango and by the famous Astor Piazzolla, among others, and considered "Argentinean", though it was designed in Germany).

This is why, with the harmonica, we must master breathing technique, legato playing, and the breath so that the fact of whether a note is blown or drawn becomes unimportant.

Now let's play the following exercise, still slowly but aiming for a certain degree of fluidity between notes.

2.7

The following exercises deal with the first jumps between non-neighboring tones. That is, notes which are not located next to each other. Moreover–and I'm repeating myself–always keep in mind the name of the note played and its position.

For example, playing an A in the middle octave means thinking not only that the note is an A, but that it's positioned on hole 7 and drawn. Unlike the piano, guitar and many others, the harmonica is not an instrument that can be looked at while playing. Therefore, it is important to be aware of which note is sounding and on which hole. Let's try putting this suggestion, which is fundamental to the study of this instrument, into practice. Turn to exercise 2.10. Remember: high C blown in hole 9, and not blown in hole 8.

The next four exercises, though quite mechanical like the preceding ones, are also melodic. For this reason, we must keep the right tempo. Count the beats of the bar mentally. If respecting the duration of the notes and rests is difficult, stop a moment and do a rhythmic and melodic solfège of the exercise before playing it on the harmonica.

The exercises must be performed slowly taking great care in giving each note and rest its proper length.

2.11

2.12

2.13

2.14

Now let's play the following two tunes. Let's respect the tempos indicated. The pieces are recorded in two different versions on the enclosed CD: one featuring only the accompaniment, the other complete with the harmonica melody.

Attention: practice the tune alone at first, without the accompaniment and without listening to the recorded harmonica. This will help train your music reading skills. Afterwards, the tune can be played along with the pre-recorded harmonica, and then with the accompaniment only.

Harmonica 1

2.15

Harmonica 2

2.16

Chapter Three

Exercises on sound and the low octave

Timbre: the voice of our instrument, the soul of our music.

After having worked on the mechanical and reading exercises of chapter 2 we'll now concentrate more on the quality of the sound we produce. In this context, sound is understood as the timbre of our instrument.

Timbre is definitely among the most important aspects for a performer.

In music, from classical to pop, from rock to jazz, from blues to world music, the great musician is first and foremost recognizable by his sound.

In jazz music, just think of Miles Davis' trumpet, so different from Chet Baker's or Dizzy Gillespie's, and Charlie Parker's alto saxophone or the unmistakable guitar of Pat Metheny. As far as our instrument is concerned, think of the wonderful and so often imitated sound of Toots Thielemans or Larry Adler or Hugo Diaz. In rock music, Jimi Hendrix's sound immediately comes to mind, or that– diametrically opposed–of Mark Knopfler or Eddy Van Halen or a thousand other guitarists. There is page after page of examples.

The importance of sound is even more understandable when it concerns the voice of a singer. How recognizable is the vocal timbre of Frank Sinatra or that of Luciano Pavarotti or Ella Fitzgerald?

To us musicians, the timbre of the instrument is like the voice of an actor: essential.

Apart from the characteristics of our instrument, its sound comes mainly from us and can be only minimally corrected by the use of effects. Good reverb (real or "reproduced" as it may be) can help, but it doesn't alter an instrument's sound color, its nature.

At the origin of a good instrument sound stands the musician above all. Let's never neglect sound in favor of speed.

There are many musicians with superb technique and great musicality whose instrument's sound absolutely does not match their skill level. Timbre can be influenced by many different variables. Some of these can be controlled and were noted in the course of the instrument's evolution; others are personal, physical or the like.

For example, the musician's physical traits, his thorax, as well as his mouth, larynx, tongue, teeth and the entire aural cavity affect the timbre of the harmonica. At this stage, we shouldn't expect to be able to thoroughly work on sound, but it is important to consider this aspect. Practicing long notes is useful for developing greater awareness of our sound on the instrument.

The next exercise presents a series of fermatas (which means we can play the notes marked with the fermata symbol for as long as wish, regardless of their actual value).

Let's hold them as long as we possibly can (between five and ten seconds). Focus on the following while playing:

- Correct breathing (see chapter 1).

- Holding the note. The sound must be clear and steady, not faint. We mustn't play the attack of the note strongly and then let it fade away.

- Listening to the sound emitted. Holding the notes long enables us to listen to our timbre. Try positioning the tongue, lips, mouth in such away to achieve the sound we like most. There is no optimal harmonica sound, only OUR sound through our instrument.

- Let's connect the notes to each other (after having played one note for a long time, switch to the next without leaving a gap).

3.1

In the previous exercise I've chosen the notes randomly; we can really play any notes we wish (in fact, I encourage you to do so). The important thing is how we perform them, bearing in mind the goal of the exercise.

Attention: this kind of exercise on sound will have to be returned to often, utilizing the notes of the first and third octave of the harmonica as well.

THE LOW OCTAVE (FIRST OCTAVE)

The following section introduces us to the notes of the low octave (first octave of a 10 or 12-hole harmonica, second octave of a 16-hole harmonica), in such a way that we can always play blown and drawn notes alternately. Also, the following exercises take three notes at a time into consideration, then four notes, always starting on a blown note.

Attention: the notes of the low octave are not easy to produce. It may happen that some notes don't properly sound for days on end. Trust me, the harmonica isn't broken! Patience is needed while we seek out the proper embouchure and correct breathing.

The notes that are typically the most difficult to play are D (hole 1) and F (hole 2).

It is imperative not to give up, even if the sound seems ugly, faint and out of tune at first. Set out from this initial sound and search patiently and willingly. It is not as simple as pressing a button; it takes time. This is the fascinating thing about all wind instruments.

Let's stay with the sound we have found, even if it's ugly, patiently holding the note. Let's not attack the notes; if they don't sound, it has nothing to do with power or air pressure.

To those who have a 16-hole harmonica, I suggest following this method book by first learning to play the second, third and fourth octaves of the 16-hole harmonica well. Once you feel more comfortable and have dedicated yourself to the first exercises involving the slide, go back and deepen your knowledge of your instrument's first octave (the lowest) using long notes.

The longer and bigger the reeds (sounding lower notes), the more difficult it becomes to have a good sound and articulate the notes well. The choice between a 16 and 12-hole harmonica is entirely up to the player's discretion. For example, Stevie Wonder always plays a 16-hole harmonica, while Toots Thielemans has almost always preferred a 12-hole, using the 16-hole on only some recordings and concerts in the '70s.

3.2

3.3

3.4

Play the same measure several times. Repetition helps refine the "mechanics" of emitting the notes. Exercise 3.5 starts on a drawn note, though the mechanics involved remain the same, while exercise 3.6 requires playing two consecutive drawn notes in the low register, one of the most complex tasks when starting to play the harmonica. We must be patient and not force the notes. We mustn't attack the reeds; otherwise they simply will not sound.

3.5

3.6

If these last exercises seem particularly difficult, take a step back and practice single low notes, alternating blown and drawn notes as illustrated in the following exercise. Try imagining the sound of the note that won't play. You have to want the note. When the note starts to sound, stay with it but without ever forcing.

It is likely that the note will be out of tune. To tune it, sound the notes while simultaneously listening to the same pitch played in tune by, for example, a keyboard. Doing so will bring forth the sound with greater determination while helping to tune it. We must imitate the pitch/sound we hear. Initially the so-called "sound beats" can be heard; that is we hear a difference in tuning between the note we play on the harmonica and the note from the keyboard. It's a kind of "wa-wa" effect which produces an actual oscillation of sound waves. We must therefore act upon our sound to minimize this "wa-wa" effect until we have one single pitch without any vibrato.

This intonation exercise will also have to be repeated in the future, on all notes of the harmonica, in order to have control over the instrument's intonation.

3.7

Then let's practice long-notes on the low octave, just like we did before on the middle octave (exercise 3.1).

Everything said about long-notes on the middle octave, applies to the low octave.

Now let's try playing a C major scale on the low octave.

3.8

The following four exercises are to be practiced meticulously, respecting the tempos indicated.

Special care must be taken with exercises 3.11 and 3.12, as they feature intervals that are difficult to play. Jumping between holes on the harmonica is always a complex operation, and repeated exercise is the means for becoming proficient.

Let's not immediately play the following exercises, 3.11 and 3.12, from beginning to end. Given the difficulty of the jumps between holes we'll practice the exercise measure by measure, doing the same jump repeatedly. For example, it is likely we'll encounter some difficulties when jumping from C to A, from C to B, and in the octave jump from C to C.

Let's take them on one at a time, repeating each interval over and over again, ascending (3.11) and descending (3.12).

3.11

3.12

Now let's play the following short tune.

It might not be the most interesting tune, but I promise that once we're past the technical issues of the first chapters, we'll play other compositions that are more inspiring.

Attention: don't forget to respect the tempos and follow the repeat signs.

Harmonica 3

TRACK 5

TRACK 6

3.13

Now we can play the tunes HARMONICA 1 (2.15) and HARMONICA 2 (2.16) of the previous chapter on the first octave–rather than on the second octave as notated. This will help us become aware of how things change from one octave to the next, both from the technical and sound perspective.

In time, our skill will be such as to perform on the entire range of the harmonica with ease, feeling no difference between the various octaves.

Often, it happens that we're reading a song in one octave but playing it in another. This occurs simply because we prefer the sound of one octave over the one notated, or because we lack some of the notated notes. For instance, if we were to play the notes of the following exercise with a 12-hole harmonica, we'd have to begin not on the actual C in hole 1, but on the C in hole 5.

3.14

JOINING NOTES OF THE FIRST AND SECOND OCTAVE

Now I'll introduce a series of exercises dealing with notes from the central and lower octaves simultaneously.

We'll begin by playing the C major scale over two octaves; from C hole 1 to C hole 9.

3.15

Now we'll play the following melodic exercises to help us join notes belonging to both octaves. As always, let's respect the length of the notes and rests. Mentally count each beat, trying to keep the tempo as constant as possible. It's important not to accelerate in the easier sections, only to slow down in difficult passages.

3.16

3.17

The following four exercises are so-called "mechanical" exercises that develop the basic technique required by our instrument. These are practiced daily on every musical instrument and help make certain passages more fluent.

It is interesting to note that after some time we will no longer notice whether we're blowing or drawing; this happens naturally and we end up thinking only of the notes.

These types of exercises can eventually be practiced on the entire range of the instrument, in all keys and at varying tempos. They are and will be a useful, necessary mechanical tool and create a foundation for the study of improvisational techniques.

In every chapter, all mechanical exercises will be marked with a small triangle like this ▲. This indicates that each time a new key is introduced in this method book, the mechanical exercises of the other keys should be practiced again as well.

For example, the following four exercises will not be transposed to the keys introduced later in this method book; step by step, they will have to be transposed to all twelve major keys, and even the minor keys.

Attention: the recommendation is that, in the end, all exercises indicated with the small triangle should eventually be practiced in all keys.

In addition, instead of performing the exercise solely in an automatic way, let's always keep in mind what note is being played and where it is located on the staff and on the instrument. The harmonica is an instrument which doesn't allow us to see the notes we play, making it easy to get lost initially. We may play a note without knowing what it is, and this causes us to lose our point of reference for playing the notes that follow. To avoid this serious problem, it is essential to ALWAYS be aware which note is being played.

I have already explained this concept, but it is necessary to repeat it to ensure a solid approach to the instrument. It is important for any instrumentalist to always know what note he/she is playing. It is like talking—one should always know the meaning of the word spoken. That said, the reality that surrounds us often contradicts us.

Attention: regardless of where the 'triangle' exercises are written, we should always try playing them over the entire range of the instrument.

Let's make the most of all the notes on our harmonica (from hole 1 to hole 12).

As I've already said, a good instrumentalist, in the long run, will feel no difference between playing high, central or low notes.

But let's not get carried away with these exercises: the notes must be cleaner and cleaner, focusing on sound, never neglecting these aspects for the sake of speed.

▲ 3.18

▲ 3.19

Now let's have fun with the next tune, Harmonica 4, written in 4/4 to simplify it for you, but which could be more interesting if played in cut time.

Are you in doubt about what cut time is? In the following chapter I'll give you a list of helpful references if you feel you're lacking knowledge of theory, harmony and solfège. A good knowledge of basic theory becomes essential if we want to play an instrument well. The need for a good basis becomes more and more evident as we continue learning the instrument.

Harmonica 4

TRACK 7
TRACK 8

3.22

Chapter Four

The high octave (third octave)

Now we'll attend to the notes of the third and final octave, the high one, which extends from C hole 9 to the highest C in hole 12. Some of these pitches were included in the last exercises we practiced.

Initially, the high notes are a little more difficult to sound. The higher they are, the shorter the reed becomes. This requires blowing and drawing a bit more intensely and bringing the lips a bit closer together (with the Whistle Method). The notes will seem a bit "harder" to sound, but this is perfectly normal.

As I mentioned earlier, on all wind instruments the notes at both the high and low ends of the range are the most difficult to play. Through exercise, this difficulty will be mastered and forgotten.

In the next exercise, let's hold the notes for as long as possible and search for the timbre we like most, just like when we began playing notes of the lower two octaves in the preceding chapters.

4.1

The next exercise is a kind of C major scale. Draw out each individual note. Two ways of notating the exercise are shown. Keep in mind that we will rarely encounter notes written so high. Often the *8va* or *"all'ottava"* marking is used to facilitate reading the notes (4.2). We also need to be able to recognize and play notes with many ledger lines (4.3).

4.2

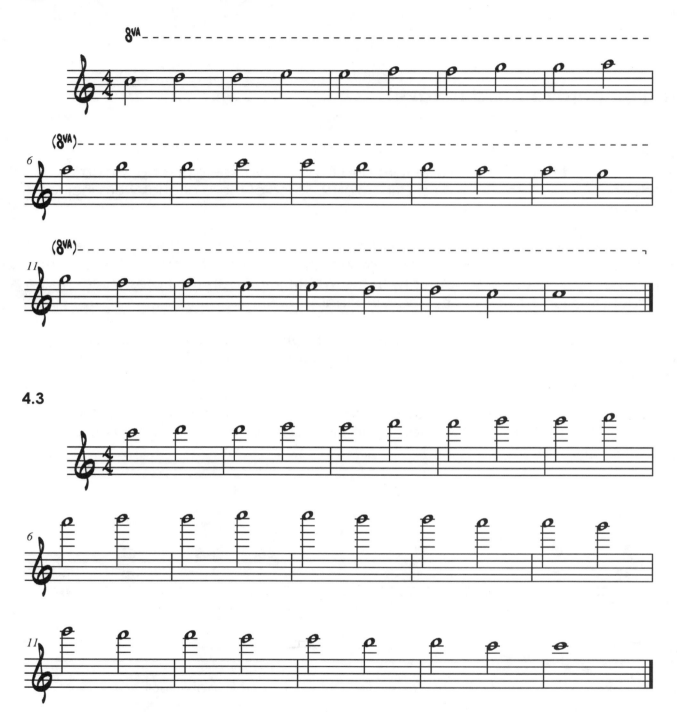

4.3

Now let's focus on the following exercise, to be played slowly, keeping in mind the note being played and its position.

4.4

Next we'll play the C major scale in the high octave only (4.5); after practicing the high octave well, we'll play it over all three octaves starting from hole 1 until hole 12 (4.6).

4.5

4.6

Let's return now to the four tunes presented in the two previous chapters (*Harmonica1*, *2*, *3* and *4*) and try playing them in the harmonica's high octave.

Initially, playing the same exercise/tune in different octaves not only gets us well acquainted with the entire range of the instrument, it allows us to hear how the same melody sounds different in various ranges.

Now on to play the following two exercises. Pay attention to the rests, especially in exercise 4.8, which will take time to play well. It's the rests that make this exercise awkward to play correctly.

As suggested before, if the rhythmic subdivision is giving us trouble, we can stop and do a rhythmic solfège of the tune.

It is never a waste of time to solfège a piece or some of its passages.

To this end, I'd like to emphasize a point which I consider of fundamental importance in the study of any musical instrument, not only the harmonica.

In my teaching experience, I've noticed that the greatest difficulty a student may have is playing a score and being exact with tempos and rests. It is mistakenly thought that the difficulty of playing notes lies only in pitch, overlooking the fact that assigning notes and rests their proper length within the tempo can be a pitfall.

When played alone or in a group, music must always have a cyclic nature.

Great care must be taken with timing, especially at the beginning of our instrumental studies. Don't interpret yet, just be precise. Don't be afraid of sounding inexpressive and pedantic. The time for interpreting music will come.

Attention: Playing written music means we take on at least three issues simultaneously:

- recognizing the length of the note or rest to be played;

- recognizing the pitch of the note to be played;

- transferring this information onto the instrument (i.e. knowing the instrument from a technical point of view)

It is not unusual to feel blocked or experience great difficulty while attempting to do these three things simultaneously. As with any complex problem, the only solution is split it into smaller issues which can be dealt with one by one.

Thus we focus first on the rhythmic subdivision of the tune through rhythmic solfège (very important phase). Then we focus on pitch through singing solfège and finally we practice it on the instrument. The procedure might seem elaborate, but it actually saves us a lot of time, allowing us to play correctly more quickly.

Only through the progressive development of a good study METHOD can better results be achieved quickly.

At the end of this chapter is a list of books which can help develop knowledge of solfège, theory and harmony.

4.7

4.8

4.9

4.10

4.11

As already mentioned, we must now pay particular attention to exercises 4.12 and 4.13. They are not simple melodic reading exercises at all; they require a good deal of attention in performance. Apart from doing some preliminary solfège, remember the importance of spending time on certain measures and passages we find more difficult. It is not necessary to always repeat the piece from the beginning; instead we must first isolate the difficult passages and then put everything together.

4.12

4.13

What follows are three mechanical exercises marked with the small triangle.

After having played them several times as notated, try them over the entire range of the instrument.

▲ 4.14

▲ 4.15

▲ 4.16

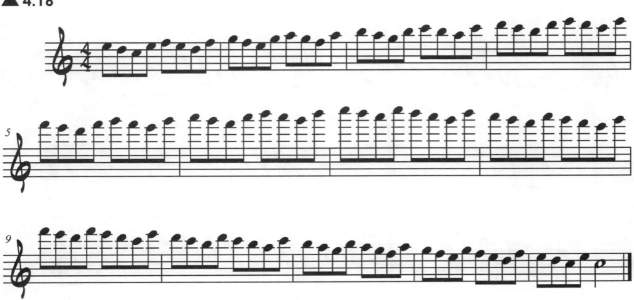

Keep in mind that studying the high octave does not end here: there will be other exercises in the following chapters to aid in playing the high notes better.

Attention: on the last hole, number 12, it will also be possible to play a D by using the slide, but we'll do this only when we've introduced the use of the slide.

What follows is a very useful exercise that, because of its importance, will be shown in other keys later on. This exercise helps develop the use of scales, starting from any degree of the scale. It's not only useful for breathing and instrumental technique; it lays the foundation for future studies on modal scales.

After having played it as notated, let's play it on the entire range of the harmonica. In the key of C, this exercise can be played over three octaves.

Remember to always play slowly (I suggest 90 beats per minute on the metronome per quarter note) and connect the notes.

This exercise is a good one to perform daily at the start of a practice routine or when warming up for a concert.

▲ 4.17

Now let's get acquainted with a new type of exercise marked with a small arrow and named after a month of the year. Although they feature melodic-harmonic development and are written in different keys, each of these exercises introduces a different basic rhythmic-melodic idea. The goal is to develop reading and performance skills through various rhythmic-melodic challenges.

January

TRACK 9
TRACK 10

➡ 4.18

Suggested books:

RHYTHMIC SOLFEGE

Solfège Rythmique Cahier n.1 – Dante Agostini – Editions Dante Agostini

Solfège Rythmique Cahier n.2 – Dante Agostini – Editions Dante Agostini

SPOKEN/SUNG SOLFEGE

The Real Easy Ear Training Book – Roberta Radley – Sher Music Co.

Ear Training for the contemporary musician – Keith Wyatt, Carl Schroeder, Joe Elliott – Hal Leonard

MUSIC THEORY

Berklee Music Theory – Paul Schmeling – Book 1and 2 (CD included) – Berklee Press

Contemporary Music Theory – Level 1, 2 and 3 – Mark Harrison – Hal Leonard

MUSIC HARMONY FOR JAZZ MUSIC

The Jazz Theory Book – Mark Levine – Sher Music Co.

Harmony & Theory – Keith Wyatt e Carl Schroeder – Hal Leonard

Mechanics of Modern Music – Anthony Zano – Ed. Berben

To further knowledge of reading exercises

Reading key Jazz Rhythm (for piano) – Fred Lipsius – Advance Music

Jazz Conception for Saxophone – Lennie Niehaus – vol. 1 (basic) – Try Publications

Jazz Conception for Saxophone – Lennie Niehaus – vol.2 (intermediate) – Try Publications

Jazz Conception for Saxophone – Lennie Niehaus – 20 jazz etudes – (advanced) – Try Publications

The technique of the flute – Rhythm Studies – Joseph Viola – Berklee Series

The technique of the flute – Scale Studies – Joseph Viola – Berklee Series

To further knowledge of exercises on arpeggios over chords (only after having studied Ch. 10)

Patterns for jazz – J. Coker, J. Casale, G. Campbell, J. Greene – ed. Alfred

The technique of the flute – Chord Studies – Joseph Viola – Berklee Series

Chapter Five

Let's use the slide

The button on the right side of the harmonica is called a slide. It is played with the right index finger using either the fleshy part of the third phalanx (near the fingertip) or the first phalanx.

Personally, I mainly use the first phalanx of my index finger for the slide and only in some cases, the fleshy part of the finger.

In my opinion, there are advantages and disadvantages to both positions but I can assure you that harmonica players will all hold differing views. The use of the fleshy part of the index finger is much more useful for playing high notes on the harmonica. By contrast, the use of the first phalanx permits a more stable hold of the harmonica. In addition, this position is more appropriate when holding a microphone for amplification.

However, I'd suggest that you choose the way that works best for you, trusting in your instincts and comfort in performance.

There are also some harmonica players who use the fleshy part of the thumb, but this position, in my view, is less stable for the instrument because both thumbs are normally used to hold the instrument.

When the slide is pushed, the note sounds one half-step higher. This works in the same way for both blown notes and drawn notes.

For example, if the note C is produced by blowing on the first hole, this means a C# or Db will sound when the slide is pressed. Or if the note F is produced by drawing on the sixth hole, it means if the slide is pressed, F# or Gb will sound. To play a flat, we have to always start one step lower and raise it up a half step with the slide. If we want to have a Db, we have to play a C#, that is, a C with the slide pressed.

By using the slide, you can automatically create enharmonic sounds. Enharmonic sounds are notes that are written differently but produce the same sound (ex: E# is enharmonic for F, Cb is enharmonic for B, etc.).

For example, F is found by drawing the 2nd, 6th and 10th holes, but it can also be found by blowing the 2nd, 6th and 10th holes with the slide (an E#). This way we have an F on the same hole that can be played drawn or blown with the slide.

We have the same note with a C blown on the 4th and 5th hole (just like on the 8th and 9th) but we discover that by using the slide, there is a drawn C on the 4th and 8th (B#).

We must be careful because the slide has no intermediate steps except for the purpose of producing particular effects. For this reason, it is important to practice being fast and, above all, precise in passing from notes needing the slide to those without.

Thanks to the slide, we are able to play in all keys.

Once the use of the slide has been established, we can play a G Major scale starting on the 3rd hole. I suggest the following: G (3 bl), A (3 dr), B (4 dr), C (5 bl), D (5 dr), E (6 bl), F# (6 dr + slide), G (7 bl). The same goes for the next octave.

Now let's continue with the G Scale over 2 octaves.

5.1

If this is too difficult, it is better to practice the scale on the first octave (from hole 3 to hole 7) repeatedly for a time. Then play the same skillfully without speeding up on the higher octave (from hole 7 to hole 11). After that, we can put the two scales together to form a two-octave scale.

ATTENTION: Here we find a new passage on the harmonica requiring practice, namely the passage E, F#, G. Let's play these 3 notes up and down as fluidly as possible in a slow tempo. You shouldn't hear spaces between one note and the other. The notes should be smooth and played uniformly without pulling on the reeds too much. You should try to play cleanly but above all, it's important to get used to the passage from F# to G. They are played in two very different positions that must eventually be performed naturally and spontaneously.

5.2

5.3

Now let's practice the following technical exercises.

 ▲ **5.4**

▲ 5.5.

▲ 5.6

Performance speed and the use of the metronome

An important element that hasn't been mentioned is the performance speed of exercises and tunes.

Until now, I have invited you to play slowly. Let's keep in mind that as you progress, once a piece has been practiced slowly, you should try to speed it up step by step, without overdoing it. How quickly you play (especially for practice purposes) is always based on your level of skill.

We should always try to keep the speed of a piece in relation to the most difficult part of that piece.

A mistake to avoid is playing at a certain speed only to slow down at the hard part.

The best thing is to isolate the group of notes or the whole bar that you find difficult and then insert it into the whole piece. If the exercise/piece is problematic, we have to practice it bar by bar, as all performers do. This is an essential focal point of this method of study.

In addition, after a piece has been practiced, a metronome can be a useful tool. The metronome itself doesn't help us resolve tempo problems. It simply gives us a reference point that helps keep us from speeding up or slowing down.

However, it is our rhythmic knowledge that makes us understand each note's duration and its relation to the tempo. Playing in time while giving each note its correct value is an essential element that calls for our utmost attention.

Don't forget, the real difficulty in "reading" and following a score is not so much playing the correct notes but playing the correct notes with the correct duration.

Piece 5.7 is not a trivial one and will take some effort to play correctly.

Exercises 5.8, 5.9, 5.10 and 5.11 are a good testing ground for our rhythmic knowledge.

5.7

5.8

5.9

5.10

February

➡ 5.11

Let's go on to the key of F Major and the related technical exercises on the scale. Be careful of the passage from Bb to C. For the time being, I suggest using C blown on the fifth hole and on ninth hole.

5.12

▲ 5.13

▲ 5.14

▲ 5.15

As I've already said in the introduction, this is a method book for the chromatic harmonica that, even though it starts with the basics and doesn't aim to enter into improvisational technique, is surely oriented toward jazz (especially after the first few chapters). We have in fact arrived at the point where it starts being important to perform musical pieces with a so-called "swing" feeling.

We'll limit ourselves to thinking that when we find two eighth notes in a row, we should play the first note on the beat longer and the second, on the upbeat, shorter and accented. Jazz has a preference for accenting weak beats (the second and fourth beats in a 4/4 measure) and upbeats as opposed to downbeats. This is an absolutely oversimplified explanation but it can at least give you a general idea. Playing with "swing feel" is a common term in jazz but with the passage of time various exceptions have developed. Playing with a "swing feel" varies from musician to musician, from type to type, from era to era. The main suggestion here is simply to listen. There is no other way. It is like trying to explain the accents and inflections in languages of people from the same country but coming from different villages, provinces and regions.

You just need to listen. Get some jazz pieces from various musicians from various historic periods. It could even be interesting to listen to the same piece, a jazz standard, played by different musicians!

On the CD for this method, I myself am trying to play in a clear way and as close as possible to the rules of jazz but, obviously, I can hear my own distinct "pronunciation".

Now let's try and play the following tunes (not technical exercises) with that in mind.

5.16

5.17

5.18 is exactly like 5.10 in G Major transposed to F Major.

It's interesting to try and play the same piece transposed, because you understand how lowering things just a step changes many things on our instrument.

5.18

5.19

5.20

March

➡ 5.21

From here on out, you will find tunes and exercises that could contain passing notes outside of the scale of reference or modulate into other keys. In addition, we'll get to know pieces marked with a little square. They are compositions I wrote for some of my CDs which I've selected for this method book's level of instruction. I hope you enjoy them. If you like them, I invite you to also listen to recordings of the original versions.

Let's begin with the piece *Anguilla* found on the CD entitled *Crocevia* (Abeat Records ABJZ 0044). The piece starts out in F Major but modulates to A Major already by the fifth measure only to wander into other keys as it develops. These modulations are very common in the jazz repertory.

■ 5.22

Anguilla

M. De Aloe

At the end of every chapter, I'll recommend a series of tunes to listen to and play in relation to the key and difficulty of the corresponding chapter. The pieces will be mainly in the jazz style. This will enable us to integrate into this method book, well-known pieces taken from the New Real Book 1, 2 and 3 (by Sher Music).

Beautiful love (Dm) – The New Real Book 1
Bernie's tune (Dm) – The New Real Book 1
But beautiful (G) – The New Real Book 1
Bye bye blackbird (F) – The New Real Book 2
Chega de saudade (Dm) – The New Real Book 1
Darn that dream (G) – The New Real Book 1
Day Dream (F)- The New Real Book 3
Desafinado (F) – The New Real Book 1
Emily (G) – The New Real Book 3
Fly me to the moon (Am) – The New Real Book 2
Here's that rainy day (G) – The New Real Book 1
Honeysuckle Rose (F)- The New Real Book 2
In a sentimental mood (Dm) – The New Real Book 3
I should care (C) – The New Real Book 1
I thought about you (F) – The New Real Book 1
I'm old fashioned (F) – The New Real Book 1
Just friends (G) – The New Real Book 3
The lamp is low (G) – The New Real Book 3
Laura (G) – The New Real Book 3
Like someone in love (C) – The New Real Book 1
Line for lyons (G) – The New Real Book 1
My romance (C) – The New Real Book 1
Nature boy (Dm) – The New Real Book 1
On the sunny side of the street (C) – The New Real Book 2
Polkadots & moonbeams (F) – The New Real Book 1
Satin doll (C) – The New Real Book 1
The shadow of your smile (3) – The New Real Book 3
St. Thomas (C) – The New Real Book 1
Take the "A" train (C) – The New Real Book 1
The way you look tonight (F) – The New Real Book 1
Unforgettable (G) – The New Real Book 2
Waltz for Debby (F) – The New Real Book 1
Yesterdays (Dm) – The New Real Book 1

Chapter Six

Exercises and tunes in D and Bb Major

Now let's look at a new key: D Major, where besides F# (holes 2 – 6 – 10 drawn with the slide) we also find C# (holes 5 – 9 - 12 blown with the slide).

As mentioned before, it is possible to sound a D, using hole 12 drawn and pushing the slide, which is the highest note in C major on the chromatic harmonica. Since hole 12 is the last one on the harmonica, it would be of no use to have another C natural drawn while pressing the slide (as happens with an analogous position in holes 4 and 8). For this reason, harmonica makers preferred adding an additional note, a D. In this way, it is possible to play a major scale of exactly three octaves in the keys of both C and C#/Db, as well as in D.

Now let's get some practice in the key of D with the scale and its corresponding technical exercises. Try playing all of them over three octaves using the harmonica's maximum range, regardless of how they're written.

When playing the scales, avoid looking at the music after the first few times. Unlike reading tunes where we have to always try and follow the score, with scales and exercises marked with ▲ we must try and memorize the passages as we play.

6.1

▲ 6.2

The following exercise is comprised of a series of eight identical repeated notes. If we play with the pursed lip technique, we can play the repeated notes by *tonguing*, that is, practically inserting the tip of the tongue into the embouchure. You can think of saying "too-too-too-too", aided by bringing the tip of your tongue between your pursed lips.

This technique, which is very common for the flute, tends to produce the sound of a "carnival trumpet" on the harmonica that could work for special effect. This is where each harmonica player's taste comes in.

Personally, I'm not so fond of the sound made by this tonguing technique on the harmonica and I prefer to play repeated notes with a sound coming more from the throat/larynx.

▲ 6.3

▲ 6.4

▲ 6.5

Here are four tunes (6.6, 6.7, 6.8, 6.9) for reading (not so simple) and then a typical melodic rhythmic tune (6.10).

6.6

6.7

6.8

6.9

April

TRACK 15
TRACK 16

➡ 6.10

Now, the tune entitled *Crocevia* subdivided in three parts, from the CD of the same name. The first and third are in C Major while the central part modulates into D Major.

■ 6.11

Crocevia

M. De Aloe

Let's move on to the key with two flats in its key signature: Bb

ATTENTION: Up until now, I've always suggested playing C by blowing into holes 5, 9 and 12. Now let's experiment with two new passages on this scale.

> Bb: hole 3 drawn with the slide
> C: hole 4drawn with the slide
> D: hole 5 drawn without the slide

> or

> Bb: hole 3 drawn with the slide
> C: hole 4 blown without the slide
> D: hole 5 drawn without the slide

(obviously, the same thing holds true for the higher octave)

Let's play these passages a few times up and down and try inserting them into the new Bb scale.

This is not to say that there is just this one way to play the scale (we can also keep playing the C blown in holes 5 and 9). It is just a suggestion. I recommend playing the scale and its exercises with C in its various positions. Each of us will choose the way that flows best for us.

TO RECAP:

There are two notes on the harmonica that can be played in different positions. These notes are:

1. F that can be played drawn on holes 2, 6 and 10 and blown with the slide (E#) on the same holes (2, 6, 10).

2. C that can be played both blown on holes 5, 9 and 12 and in two other positions: on holes 4 and 8 blown without the slide and drawn with the slide.

ATTENTION: these are alternate positions and it is up to us as harmonica players to choose which position to use based on what technically seems more in keeping with the passage we're dealing with.

What follows next is the scale and its exercise 6.13.

6.12

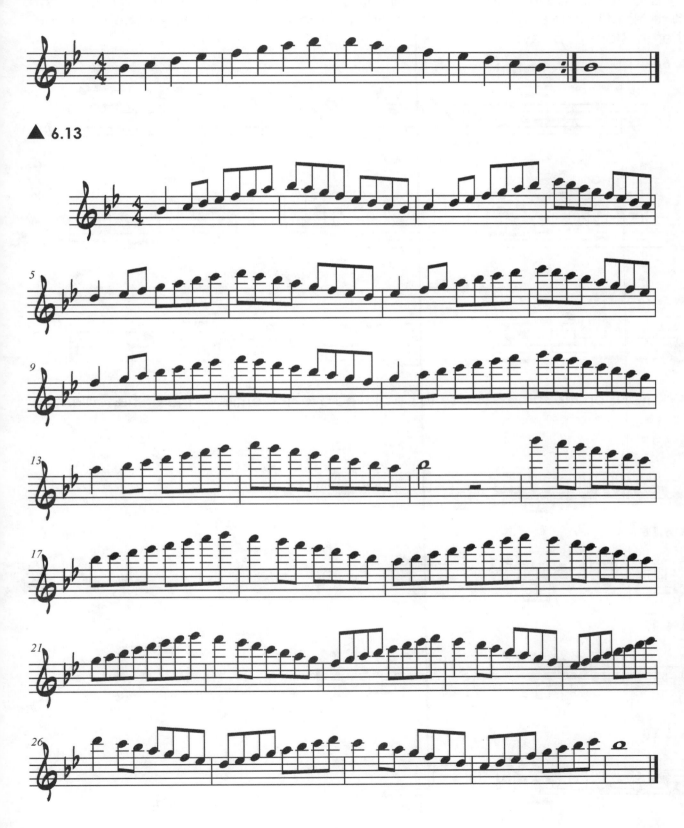

▲ 6.13

6.14 is to be played in different ways following the five variations presented here. This is a series of very useful exercises which aid in managing various intervals between the different steps of a key.

▲ **6.14**

VARIATIONS on the same exercise to be played over the entire range of the scale.

▲ **6.15**

▲ **6.16**

▲ **6.17**

▲ **6.18**

Now we will see some rhythmic variations with the following exercise. Play it without a metronome and then with, gradually speeding it up. We can begin with a tempo of 80 beats per minute and accelerate from there.

6.19

Bb Blues

6.20

The following tune, May, was written over the chords of the famous Autumn Leaves but in 3/4 time. Let's first practice the theme of Autumn Leaves in the New Real Book 1. To conclude, I'm presenting you with my tune *Partiamo all'alba*, from the 2010 CD Bradipo (Abeat ABJZ0070) and *Björk on the moon* (Abeat ABJZ 0105), the title track from the 2012 CD.

May

➡️ 6.21

TRACK 17
TRACK 18

■ 6.22

Partiamo All'alba

M. De Aloe

■ 6.23

Björk on the Moon

M. De Aloe

Suggested tunes for this chapter:

A child is born (Bb) – The New Real Book 2
Almost like being in love (Bb) – The New Real Book 3
Autumn leaves (Gm) – The New Real Book 1
Basin Street Blues (Bb) – The New Real Book 1
Come Sunday (Bb) – The New Real Book 1
Elm (Gm) – The New Real Book 1
Everything happens to me (Bb) – The New Real Book 1
I'm all smiles (D) – The New Real Book 1
In your own sweet Way (Bb) – The New Real Book 2
It don't mean a thing (Bb) – The New Real Book 2
Manha de carnival (Gm) – The New Real Book 2
A quiet place (D) – The New Real Book 2
Someday my prince will come (Bb) – The New Real Book 1
There is no greater love (Bb) – The New Real Book 2
Tristeza (D) – The New Real Book 2
Up jumped spring (Bb) – The New Real Book 1
Wave (D) – The New Real Book 1
You must believe in spring (D) – The New Real Book 3

Chapter Seven

Exercises and tunes in A and Eb Major

This chapter is structured exactly like the last two, with an emphasis on exercises and tunes in two new keys: A and Eb.

At first, working with keys richer in sharps and flats can cause a few more problems but it is just a matter of getting accustomed to them and practicing them. While practicing, we should not necessarily favor only simpler keys but concentrate more on troublesome passages presented by the new sharps and flats.

In the key of A major, more care is taken to play through the notes E-F#-G#-A smoothly.

The first four exercises (7.1, 7.2, 7.3, and 7.4) deal with the scale and technical exercises in the key of A Major.

Remember to play through step by step all the technical exercises we have encountered until now and we'll encounter in the two keys of this chapter, too.

Let's not neglect technique in favor of just playing pieces that are more pleasurable to perform.

7.1

We can observe how varying the key of the same exercises changes the passages, the position of the sharps and flats, the order of the holes and the alternating of blown and drawn notes. Playing the same passages in different keys on our instrument causes many changes. For this reason, separate practice time should be devoted to each key.

▲7.2

▲ 7.3

The following technical exercise focuses on the performance of large intervals in the key of F# minor (that is the relative minor of A Major).

It requires a good deal of attention. After having played it carefully, try and replicate it in the keys that we've encountered so far.

 7.4

Now let's play close attention what follows (7.5 and 7.6). It won't be easy to play and it's best to handle it measure by measure, concentrating on the single triplets. Be careful of the double sharps, the flats and other alterations in the key. These are followed by *June*, in A Major, built over the harmony of the jazz standard *Out of Nowhere* (normally played in G Major, however).

7.5

7.6

June

TRACK 19
TRACK 20

➡ 7.7

Now on to the key of Eb, with its corresponding first exercises on the scale.

7.8

▲ **7.9**

▲ 7.10

▲ 7.11

7.12

Eb Blues

The next exercise is in D Major, 6.9, transposed up a half step into Eb. As in Chapter 5 with exercise 5.18, the aim is to demonstrate how tricky playing the same exact thing transposed into another key can be. Let's try and play it and then go back and tackle 6.9.

7.13

7.14

Tango Fuori Stagione

M. De Aloe

The preceding tune *Tango Fuori Stagione* and the one following it, *Aliando*, can both be found on the CD *Racconti Controvento* (Abeat Records ABJZ 003 from 2001).

■ 7.15

Aliando

M. De Aloe

July is composed over the same harmonic line as the preceding tune *Aliando*.

July

TRACK 21
TRACK 22

➡ 7.16

Suggested tunes for this chapter:

Baby, It's cold outside (Eb) – The New Real Book 2
Blue Bossa (Cm) – The New Real Book 1
Blue Moon (Eb) – The New Real Book 3
Dindi (Eb) – The New Real Book 1
For all we know (Eb) – The New Real Book 3
The gentle rain (Cm) – The New Real Book 3
Gush (F#m) – The New Real Book 3
I fall in love too easily (Eb) – The New Real Book 3
Imagination (Eb) – The New Real Book 1
Moonlight in Vermont (Eb) – The New Real Book 1
Misty (Eb) – The New Real Book 1
Once I loved (A) – The New Real Book 1
Out of this world (Eb) – The New Real Book 1
Over the rainbow (Eb) – The New Real Book 3
Reincarnation of a lovebird (F#m) – The New Real Book 1
Sing me softly of the blues (A) – The New Real Book 2
Skylark (Eb) – The New Real Book 1
Someone to light up my life (A) – The New Real Book 2
Solar (Cm) – The New Real Book 1
Solitude (Eb) – The New Real Book 3
Speak no evil (Cm) – The New Real Book 1
Tenderly (Eb) – The New Real Book 1
There will never be another you (Eb) – The New Real Book 1
These foolish things (Eb) – The New Real Book 1
Triste (A) – The New Real Book 1

The next chapter is entirely dedicated to scales. For each key, you will find the major scale and its relative minor. In addition, pentatonic and blues scales in both major and minor keys are presented here.

It isn't necessary to practice all the scales presented here before going on to Chapter 9, but it is a good idea to at least practice all the major scales. The pentatonic and blues scales are a first step toward the technique of improvisation and should certainly peak our curiosity.

Chapter Eight

Scales

C

C major

A natural minor

A melodic minor

A jazz melodic minor

A harmonic minor

C major pentatonic

A minor pentatonic

C major blues

A minor blues

G

G major

E natural minor

E melodic minor

E jazz melodic minor

E harmonic minor

G major pentatonic

E minor pentatonic

G major blues

E minor blues

D

A

A major

F# natural minor

F# melodic minor

F# jazz melodic minor

F# harmonic minor

A major pentatonic

F# minor pentatonic

A major blues

F# minor blues

E

E major

C#natural minor

C# melodic minor

C# jazz melodic minor

C# harmonic minor

E major pentatonic

C# minor pentatonic

E major blues

C# minor blues

B

F

F major

D natural minor

D melodic minor

D jazz melodic minor

D harmonic minor

F major pentatonic

D minor pentatonic

F major blues

D minor blues

Bb

Bb major

G natural minor

G melodic minor

G jazz melodic minor

G harmonic minor

Bb major pentatonic

G minor pentatonic

Bb major blues

G minor blues

Eb

Eb major

C natural minor

C melodic minor

C jazz melodic minor

C harmonic minor

Eb major pentatonic

C minor pentatonic

Eb major blues

C minor blues

Ab

Ab major

F natural minor

F melodic minor

F jazz melodic minor

F harmonic minor

Ab major pentatonic

F minor pentatonic

Ab major blues

F minor blues

Db

Gb

Gb major

Eb natural minor

Eb melodic minor

Eb jazz melodic minor

Eb harmonic minor

Gb major pentatonic

Eb minor pentatonic

Gb major blues

Eb minor blues

Chapter Nine

The other keys

Now we can dedicate ourselves to the remaining five keys: E, Ab, B, Db and Gb.
Exercise 4.17 was not written in these five keys but can be used as a preparatory
exercise transported into whichever key we're dealing with. Let's begin with E Major.

▲ 9.1

▲ 9.2

9.3 is exactly like 7.5 in A Major transposed in E Major.

9.3

9.4 has many rhythmic variations and some not-so-simple technical passages. Then comes the rhythmic melodic tune *August,* written over the well-known standard jazz harmony from *There will never be another you* (but usually played in the key of Eb Major).

9.4

August

TRACK 23
TRACK 24

➡ 9.5

Now let's go on to the key of Ab. Following the technical exercise 9.6, we can play the tune *Nel Golfo Mistico* from the 2008 CD *Lirico Incanto* (Abeat records ABJZ 0060).

Remember to always take advantage of the tips found at the end of each chapter about jazz standards that can be played in the various keys we are focusing on.

▲ 9.6

■ 9.7

Nel Golfo Mistico

M. De Aloe

Now another tune from my CD, *Ul Giuan Marcora* from the aforementioned *Crocevia*. To be more precise, this tune is played by an accordion on the CD but it doesn't matter. It can be played as a tango-cancion or also works as a slow bossa nova. The important thing is to highlight its melancholic, nostalgic character. In this type of number, we can bring out the sound of our instrument, digging deep on some notes and playing with the dynamics.

Remember to never play everything at the same volume. Dynamics have an important role in what we're playing. Think of an actor reciting lines and think of how much value the tone of his voice adds to the meaning of the words. The same holds true for music.

Ul Giuan Marcora

M. De Aloe

September

TRACK 25
TRACK 26

➡ 9.9

Now let's tackle the key of B Major. 9.10 is to be played in various modalities using the following four variations.

▲ 9.10

▲ 9.11

▲ 9.12

▲ 9.13

▲ 9.14

9.15

October

➡ 9.16

The key of D flat Major is next. For these new keys, remember to return to the technical exercises we did in the preceding keys.

After exercise 9.17, which highlights intervals of a fifth, we find a Bb minor blues (9.18) and a little tune (9.19). After that we find the rhythmic melodic tune *November*, composed over the harmonies of the jazz standard *Body & Soul*. This famous ballad was written in 1930 by Johnny Green and made famous by the greats of jazz (Ella Fitzgerald, Billie Holiday, Coleman Hawkins, John Coltrane, Keith Jarrett, Sonny Rollins; etc.).

▲ **9.17**

9.18

Bb Minor Blues

9.19

November

➡ 9.20

Next comes the final key of F sharp Major with 6 sharps in the key signature and enharmonic with G flat with 6 flats in its key signature. We finish with 9.23 and then with the rhythmic melodic tune *December*, this, too written over the harmonies of another well-known jazz standard: *Take Five*, composed by Paul Desmond and made famous by the Dave Brubeck Quartet.

▲ 9.21

▲ 9.22

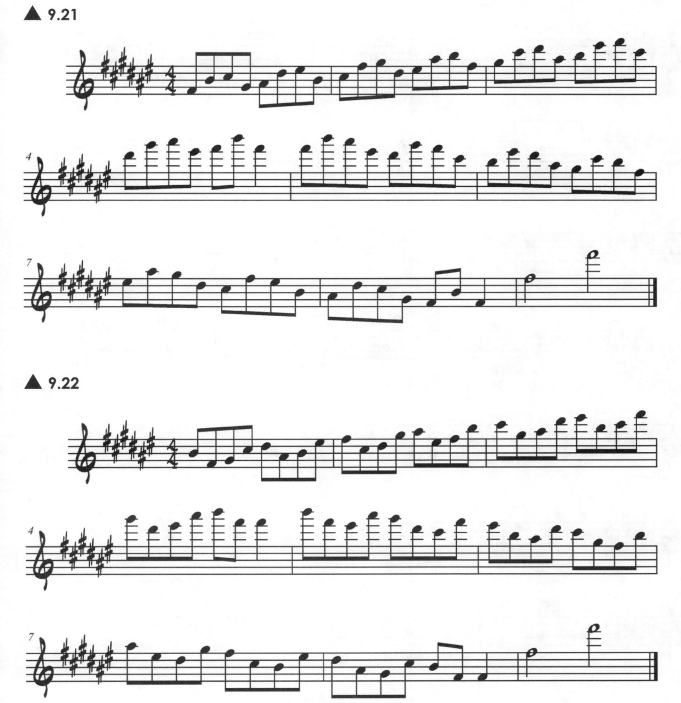

9.23

December

TRACK 31
TRACK 32

➡ 9.24

At this point, it seems important to touch on two topics that are very essential in the study of the harmonica, namely vibrato and bending.

VIBRATO

The subject of vibrato is generally a very complex one, in part because it brings to mind stylistic, interpretive and historical differences and their consequent technical difficulties.

In wind instruments which have a solid tradition of performance and instruction, there are various schools of thought on how to carry out this technique. However, with the harmonica, keep in mind that we are faced with two fundamental challenges: one, the lack of didactic material for our instrument; and two, the fact that it is the only instrument which produces sounds by both blowing and drawing air. One thing we can do is to attempt to modify for the harmonica certain techniques taken from other wind instruments.

Before we begin, what is vibrato? Vibrato is a light undulating fluctuation that acts on the timbre, dynamic and very subtly on the intonation of our sound. Vibrato is produced on a note by slightly altering the emission (or drawing in) of air. The easiest way to vibrate a note is to move the actual instrument while playing a particular note. I feel compelled to advise against this technique. No other wind instrument player vibrates by moving his instrument, yet on the harmonica, it is often done because it's easy to do. That said, this type of vibrato can be very interesting for those who play the diatonic harmonica. Another way I'd advise against doing vibrato on the chromatic harmonica is by moving the right hand close to and away from the instrument case.

I'd now like to recommend two other vibrato techniques called **diaphragmatic** and **laryngeal** (also defined as throat vibrato). For these two modalities, let's concentrate on one blown note. When we are able to vibrate one or more blown notes, we can go on and develop the same technique on drawn notes. It's important to take into account that passing from blown to drawn vibrato calls for yet another skill.

With **diaphragmatic vibrato**, our starting point is the same logic as diaphragmatic sound emission (chap. 1), getting accustomed to sounding slightly accented notes so that the air pressure undergoes minute variations. Play triplets on the same note, first slowly and then faster and faster. The aim here is to have all these note repetitions on the same hole give a single sound that oscillates just enough to produce a vibration. These triplets must absolutely not be played by tonguing but rather by "pulsing" with the diaphragm.

In the end, we should produce a constant, undulating sound with no sudden lurches. Keep in mind that the process is a long one and requires a great deal of patience. It is not enough to simply try it a few times. Time and practice are essential.

Laryngeal vibrato is produced thanks to the muscles of the larynx which also has among its many functions, that of regulating the opening of the glottis. By alternating opening and closing the glottis, a vibrating effect is created in the note being played. To make a good laryngeal vibrato, it's important to be free from unnecessary muscular tension in the neck area and around the larynx in particular.

Laryngeal vibrato is often mistakenly avoided because it is said to create a bleating effect, so much so that the French defined this type of vibrato as *chevrotment* (from *chevre*, goat). But attention – this type of vibrato can be performed very well to wonderful effect if we manage to not create too much tension in the throat; such tension tightens the undulating movement of the larynx. Let's not dismiss it outright. It becomes "bleating" only if done poorly. The same steps are taken with this vibrato as with the diaphragmatic vibrato: short notes repeated over and over become a single vibrated sound.

Often, breathing from the diaphragm can be glorified, but let's not forget that everything can contribute to "our sound" in accordance with our particular taste.

The subject of vibrato, as you've probably sensed, is extremely varied and as such, I've limited myself to dealing with it in these few lines about the basics. For those interested in furthering their knowledge of the subject, it is useful to find texts and exercises in flute methods such as Trevor Wye and James Galway. There is a vast literature regarding vibrato.

In conjunction with vibrato, I feel I want to make some final concluding thoughts.

- Before trying vibrato, we must have attained an excellent tone and decent technique.

- Sound is not always improved with the use of vibrato. Miles Davis, for example, created a musical sound completely free of vibrato and the same goes for many jazz players and musicians in general who have chosen the same path.

- Listen to all kinds of vibrato, effects and embellishments of other harmonica players and instrumentalists and try and understand where to focus your efforts. What type of vibrato do you like? Where to use it? Remember that the words written in this method book are of little use if they are cut off from the marvelous music that exists and those who performer it. Every great musician we listen to is a valuable teacher for each of us.

- While we're doing the vibrato exercises, it is vital to want to play them not only with the breath, the diaphragm, the throat or whatever else but also with the head. Imagine the vibrated note.

- In addition, let's remember that all the effects we can produce (vibrato, trills, tonguing, guttural sounds, bending, etc.) vary greatly depending on whether we're playing a chromatic or diatonic harmonica and depending on the different types of music. Just think of how different Toots Thielemans' vibrato is from Franz Chmel's. Harmonica instruction mustn't be reduced to a single model or a single sound.

BENDING

Bending is another very important subject for harmonica players.

Bending is an effect that allows us to modify the intonation of a note resulting in an impressive "sliding sound". Bending is of the utmost importance for those playing the diatonic harmonica. In fact, the diatonic harmonica makes up for its lack of all 12 notes of the chromatic scale by using bending and overbending to move notes a half-step, and in some cases, a whole-step or even a step and a half. This is done through the use of a particular technique that creates a kind of vortex of air that blocks the reed that we're drawing, for example, and sounds the reed that normally only sounds when blown. This subject is beyond the scope of this method book, as this type of bending cannot be done on the chromatic harmonica because, unlike the diatonic harmonica, the valves positioned on each reed act as an obstacle to producing this type of effect.

Bending on the chromatic harmonica has the principal aim of slightly lowering the intonation of the note that is being played, giving it a distinctive effect. In both blown and drawn notes, these elements apply:

- the tip of the tongue is arched and moved downward which consequently swells the inner part of the tongue more.

- the larynx is lowered (think of yawning)

- the entrance or exit of air is slightly forced

To do a bend on a drawn note, the larynx has to be lowered much more than when blowing. Touch your Adam's apple while inhaling; start forcing the air a bit to make a bend and you should clearly feel your Adam's apple drop.

As with vibrato, bending will become a very personal technique which each of us must do in the most functional way, both musically and technically, depending on the shape of our oral cavity.

There are countless variables in esthetic and stylistic dictates regarding the quality of bending.

Listen to what you like and try and follow that road until you are capable of creating your own personal version of it. In fact, after firmly establishing skills on our instrument (reading musical rhythms and melodies, instrumental technique, timbre, etc), we can begin thinking about interpreting the music. Bear in mind that while many strengths will spring from our way of playing, some of our weaknesses emerge as well, and they, too, can become a way to set our "musical art" apart. There is no "right" way of making a sound or doing embellishments, otherwise we would all play in the same exact way with the same exact sound. As I outlined in the introduction to this method book, we should listen to the sound and technique of other instruments. Then, after reaching a certain level, we can share musical experiences with others. It's fine to play to playbacks or sequencers, but playing with others teaches us so much.

We should never be afraid to play with musicians better than us.
The three basic elements a musician cannot disregard are:

- listening to plenty of music (don't be lazy – go and listen to concerts)

- practicing his own instrument

- playing with others

Suggested tunes for this chapter:

Airegin (Fm) – The New Real book 1
Along came Betty (Ab) – The New Real Book 2
Body and soul (Db) – The New Real Book 2
Chelsea bridge (Db) – The New Real Book 1
Django (Fm) – The New Real Book 2
Falling Grace (Ab) – The New Real Book 2
Isfahan (Db) – The New Real Book 2
Naima (Ab) – The New Real Book 2
So many stars (Db) – The New Real Book 2
Sophisticated lady (Ab) – The New Real Book 2
Stardust (Db) – The New Real Book 2
Caravan (Fm) – The New Real Book 3
Dancing in the street (E) – The New Real Book 3
In a mellow tone (Ab) – The New Real Book 3
A little tear (Db) – The New Real Book 1
Lonely woman (Gb) – The New Real Book 3
Lush life (Db) – The New Real Book 1
Part-time lover (Db) – The New Real Book 3
Smile please (E) – The New Real Book 3
Stompin' at the Savoy (Db) – The New Real Book 3
That girl (B) – The New Real Book 3
Three views of a secret (E) – The New Real Book 1
What's love got to do with it (B) – The New Real Book 3

More on jazz improvisation:

The Jazz Theory Book – Mark Levine – Sher Music Co.
How to Improvise – Hal Crook – Advance Music
The Serious Jazz Practice Book – Barry Finnerty – Sher Music Co.
Elements of the Jazz Language for the Developing Improviser – Jerry Coker – Warner
Jazz Improvisation – George Bouchard – Ed. Jamey Aebersold
The Blues Scales – Dan Greenblatt – Sher Music Co.
The Real Easy Book – vol. 1 – 2 and 3 – Sher Music Co.

Transcribed solos of famous jazz musicians are also fundamental. Try and transcribe them directly from the CD (there are programs online that make it easier to transcribe by cutting the performance speed in half without changing the key).

These transcription books are a must:

Charlie Parker Omnibook – Atlantic Music Corp. (C key)
Miles Davis – Kind of blue – Hal Leonard
The Chet Baker Collection – Hal Leonard

Chapter Ten

Exercises on arpeggios and basic chords

It isn't possible to study a musical instrument without also studying chords. Chords make up the harmonic fabric of a composition. For all monophonic instruments, an in-depth study of melody and rhythm are a prerequisite to the study of chromatic harmony, and that is what we have be doing up until now.

Those who play harmonic instruments (piano, guitar, accordion, vibraphone, etc.) know how much skill is required for practicing chords. The study of chords and their harmonic relation is central, above all, in the field of jazz. However, serious study of a monophonic instrument cannot omit this topic, and the student must in time be able to recognize chords and know how to "arpeggiate" them melodically.

These exercises are arpeggios over the most important chords. It will be up to us to get to know other types of chords, step by step, over time. The first step is to begin to arpeggiate major triads.

Let's begin with exercise 10.1. The C Major triad.

Attention: it is not only important to recognize a chord by reading it; we must also memorize the notes that comprise the chord.

Let's start practicing all the 12 major triads. We must learn what notes they're made up of and be able to play them on our instrument.

Much time must be dedicated to the first three exercises of this chapter because they will then be played in the other 11 keys. After these preliminary exercises, we can now get to the heart of this chapter.

10.1

10.2

10.3

All of the following exercises demonstrate one type of arpeggio over the first three chords; with only the chord symbols of the next chord to follow, we must be able to play all the remaining arpeggios on our own.
This is a very useful type of exercise and its scope is twofold:

- to aid us technically

- to initiate us into the study of the basic chords that will later help us approach improvisational jazz technique

As I've already written, this book is not concerned with improvisational jazz technique but will certainly lay out the basics for approaching it and acquiring the necessary technical skills. With a pencil, we could mark down the metronome speed we're able to play each exercise at. Next, as we gradually increase the speed, we can find the point where we start having problems and work there on our "breaking point" until we're able to execute the exercise with ease. Then, day after day, we can go on to play faster tempos. Marking the increase in speed after days, months and even years, helps us track our progress.

This is important for focusing on technique. If we notice that we have more difficulty only in certain keys, then we can spend time on the arpeggios in that particular key. We can work technically on the arpeggio that gives us more difficulty and then reinsert it into the whole exercise.

10.4

Now let's begin studying 12 minor triads.

We can use 10.1, 10.2 and 10.3 as preliminary exercises on the minor chord.
After thoroughly practicing them, they can be applied to the next exercises.

10.8

10.9

10.10

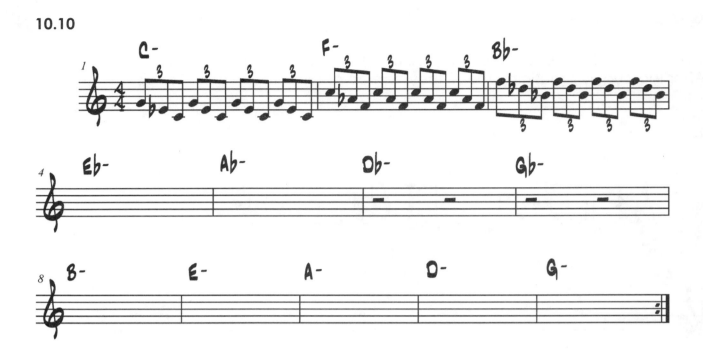

At this point, I recommend playing the exercises till now in this chapter with augmented and diminished triads as well.

Now let's find out the most common types of 4-note chords.
At first, it is necessary to practice the individual chord, just as we did with the major and minor triads.

The next exercise, 10.11, gives us a feel for a 4-note chord. Let's transpose this exercise into the various keys and the various types of chords: major triads with a major 7 – major triads with a minor 7 – minor triads with a minor 7 – half-diminished (diminished triads with a minor 7) and diminished (diminished triad with a diminished 7).

10.11

ATTENTION: never favor speed over precision. We should never lose control of our dynamics and sound.

10.12

10.13

10.14

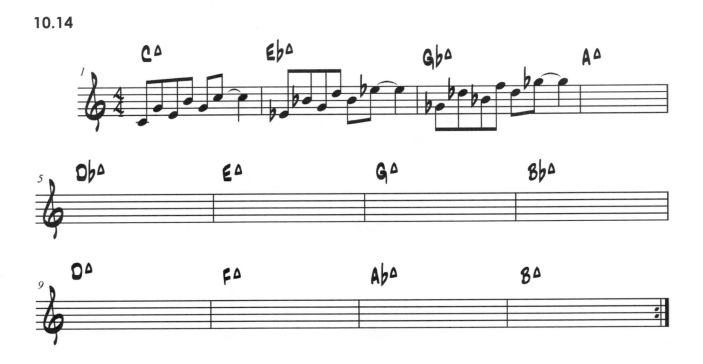

10.15

10.16

10.17

10.18

10.19

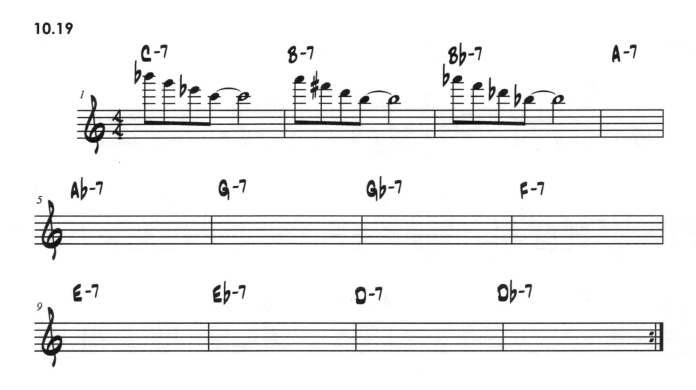

10.23

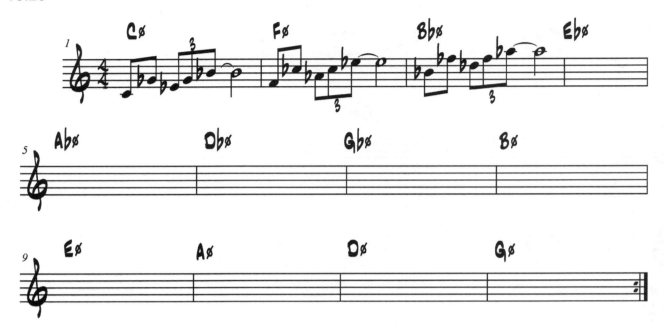

10.24

10.25

10.26

10.27

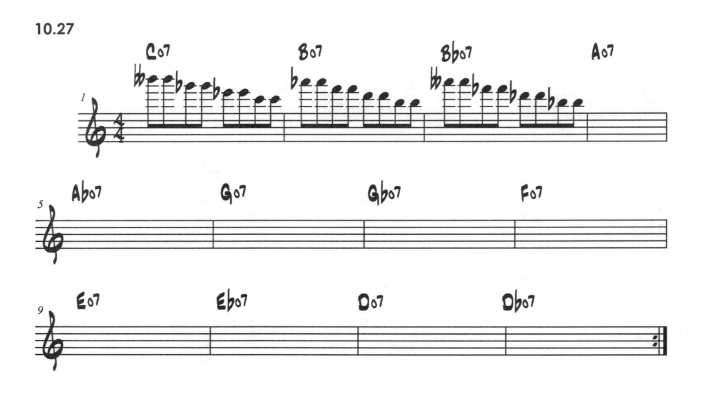

10.28

Select Discography of CDs of Chromatic Harmonica

JAZZ

TOOTS THIELEMANS – Man Bites Harmonica – Riverside
TOOTS THIELEMANS – Footprints – Emarcy
TOOTS THIELEMANS – Only trust your heart – Concord Jazz
TOOTS THIELEMANS – For my lady – Emarcy
TOOTS THIELEMANS – Harmonica Jazz – Columbia
TOOTS THIELEMANS – Chez Toots – Private Music
TOOTS THIELEMANS – Live in the Netherlands – Pablo
TOOTS THIELEMANS – European Quartet, live – Challenge
TOOTS THIELEMANS & KENNY WERNER – Thielemans & Werner – Emarcy
TOOTS THIELEMANS & BILL EVANS – Affinity – Warner Bros.
TOOTS THIELEMANS & FRED HERSCH – Concerto pour Harmonica – Tob Music
TOOTS THIELEMANS – DVD – Toots Thielemans in New Orleans

STEVIE WONDER – Eivets Rednow – Alfie – Motown

LARRY ADLER – Maestro of the Mouth Organ (The Thirties) – Asv
LARRY ADLER – The Glory of Gershwin – Island Mercury
LARRY ADLER – The Golden Era – Pegasus
LARRY ADLER – Live at the Ballroom – Newport Classic

JERRY ADLER – The Harmonica magic of Jerry Adler – Usa Music Group

CLAUDE GARDEN – Garden Club – Elabeth

BORRAH MINEVITCH – Borrah Minevitch & his Harmonica Rascals – Jasmine

TRIO RAISNER – Harmonica & big band – Vintange Music

HENDRIK MEURKENS – Slidin' – Concord Jazz
HENDRIK MEURKENS – A view from Manhattan – Concord Jazz
HENDRIK MEURKENS – New York Nights – Challenge
HENDRIK MEURKENS – Celebrando – Zoho Music

WILLIAM GALLISON – Calling you – Verve Forecast
WILLIAM GALLISON – Line Open – Waking Up
WILLIAM GALLISON & MADELEINE PEYROUX – Got you on my mind – Waking Up
MAURICIO EINHORN – Conversa de Amigos – Delira

OLIVIER KER OURIO' – Central Park Nord – Pee Wee
OLIVIER KER OURIO' – Oversea – Dreyfus Jazz
OLIVIER KER OURIO' – Siroko – Emotive Records
OLIVIER KER OURIO' – A ride with the wind – Naive

GREGOIRE MARET – Scenarios – Obliqsound
GREGOIRE MARET – Gregoire Maret – Entertainment One Music

MIKE TURK – Turk's Works – TinSandwich Music
MIKE TURK – The Nature of things – TinSandwichMusic
MIKE TURK – A Little taste of Cannonball – Organ music

JON ERIKSEN – Talkin' To Myself – Guacamole Records

HERMINE DEURLOO – Crazy Clock – Tin Wood Music
HERMINE DEURLOO – Soundbite – Earforce Records
HERMINE DEURLOO – Glass Fish – Challenge Records

LE MONDE DE KOTA – Murmures – Radar

BILL BARRETT – Gut Puppet 4 – Woetone Records

ENRICO GRANAFEI – In search of the third dimension – Miles High

DAMIEN MASTERSON – Intercambio – GoodOmen

BRUNO DE FILIPPI – In New York with Don Friedman Trio – Carosello
BRUNO DE FILIPPI – You and the night and the music – Carosello
BRUNO DE FILIPPI – You my love – Giant of Jazz

ALBERTO BORSARI – Alfonsina y el mar – Polygram

LUIGI FERRARA – Another day – Philology

FEDERICO BERTELLI – Harmonitaly – SpiritoJazz

ANGELO ADAMO – My Foolish Harp – Red Records

ANTONIO SERRANO & FEDERICO LECHNER – Sesion Continua – Nuevos Medios
ANTONIO SERRANO & JOSHUA EDELMAN TRIO – En el Central – Museek Flazz

JENS BUNGE – Shangai Blue – Rodenstein Records
JENS BUNGE – With all my heart – Yvp Music
ADAM GLASSER – Free at first – SunnySide Records

TANGO

HUGO DIAZ – Tangos – Acqua Records
HUGO DIAZ – Tango compilation – EMI

FRANCO LUCIANI – Armonica y tango – AQ
FRANCO LUCIANI – Acuarelas de bolsillo – AQ
FRANCO LUCIANI – Armusa – Acqua Records

ANTONIO SERRANO – Armonitango – Msi Music

LUIS SALTOS – A Hugo Diaz – Random Records

JOE POWERS – Amor de tango – Joe Powers records

GIANLUCA LITTERA – Sconcertango – Zone di musica

BRASIL

TOOTS THIELEMANS & ELIS REGINA – Aquarela do Brasil – Philips
TOOTS THIELEMANS – The Brasil Project – vol.1 – Private Music
TOOTS THIELEMANS – The Brasil Project – vol.2 – Private Music

GABRIEL GROSSI – Arapuca – Delira Musica
GABRIEL GROSSI – Diz que fui por aì – Phantom
GABRIEL GROSSI – Horizonte – DG
GABRIEL GROSSI & MARCO PEREIRA – Afinidade

MAURICIO EINHORN – Travesssuras – Delira Musica
MAURICIO EINHORN & SEBASTIAO TAPAJOS – Einhorn & Tapajos – Polygram Barclay

HERMINE DEURLOO & INSUNZA – Sozinhos – Jazz between the Dikes Records

HENDRIK MEURKENS – Sambahia – Concord Picante
HENDRIK MEURKENS – October Colors – Concord Picante
HENDRIK MEURKENS – Sambatropolis – Zoho Music

VITOR LOPES – Chorando as Pitangas – Lopes
VITOR LOPES & UM TRIO VIRALATA – Viragem – Penvenan

CLASSICAL MUSIC

JOHN SEBASTIAN – Harmonica Concertos – Urania

ROBERT BONFIGLIO – Romances – High Harmony
ROBERT BONFIGLIO – Villa Lobos Harmonica Concerto – RCA
ROBERT BONFIGLIO – Harmonica Classics – Bonfiglio Record

TOMMY REILLY – Harmonica Concertos & Virtuoso works – Chandos
TOMMY REILLY – Walton, Grainger, Smetana, Borodin, Arnold – BBC Radio Classic
TOMMY REILLY – Serenade – Chandos
TOMMY REILLY – Serenade vol. 2 – Chandos
TOMMY REILLY – Works for harmonica and orchestra – Chandos

WILLI BURGER – Classical Chromarmonica – Eucled
WILLI BURGER – Concerto – Eucled
WILLI BURGER – French Compositions – Eucled
WILLI BURGER – Music form Spain and South America – Eucled
WILLI BURGER – Harmonica – Activ Classics

LARRY ADLER – Genius of Larry Adler – Decca
LARRY ADLER – Harmonica Virtuso – Legacy
LARRY ADLER – Larry Adler in concert – Emi classics

FRANZ CHMEL – Fantasia Baroque – PSB
FRANZ CHMEL – Classic Harmonica vol.1 – Chmel
FRANZ CHMEL – Classic Harmonica vol 2 – Chmel
FRANZ CHMEL – Classic Harmonica vol3 – Chmel

SIGMUND GROVEN – Philharmonica – Simax Classics
SIGMUND GROVEN – Grieg Album – Grappa Records
SIGMUND GROVEN & IVER KLEIVE – Harmorgan – Simax Classics

YASUO WATANI – Harmonica Nostalgia

KING'S HARMONICA QUINTET – King's Harmonica Quintet – KHQ CD 03

JAMES HUGHES – James Hughes plays James Moody – Grosvenor

GIANLUCA LITTERA – Villa Lobos Harmonica concerto – BMG

CLAUDE GARDEN – Ambiance Classique Vol. 1 – ILD

CLAUDE GARDEN – Ambiance Classique Vol. 2 – ILD
CLAUDE GARDEN – Ambiance Classique Vol. 3 – ILD

VARIOUS

BRENDAN POWER – Plays the music from Riverdance – Greentrax
BRENDAN POWER – State of the harp – Jayrem Records

SVANG – arruta – Aito Records
SVANG – Svang – Aito Records

HAZMAT MODINE – Bahamut – Barbès Records – world

CLINT HOOVER – Dream of the serpent dog – Mr Bipps Records

PHILIP ACHILLE with MELINDA HUGHES – Smoke and noise – Nimbus

JAMES HUGHES (with Philip Achille) – A Taste of summer wine – Tasman Records

THE ADLER TRIO – Harmonicadence – Adler
THE ADLER TRIO – The Adlers live – Adler

These are some of the recordings I've had the pleasure of listening to and feel I can recommend. I'm certain there are more excellent CDs of the chromatic harmonica out there, just as I'm certain there are even more great performers that I've yet to discover. The internet makes it easier to go searching for old and new talented players, making fascinating music on this wonderful instrument. Perhaps, before long, you may be among them.

It is my hope that this method book has helped you and that you've also had fun using it.

Enjoy the music.

Max

SHER MUSIC CO. — *The finest in Jazz & Latin Publications*

THE NEW REAL BOOK SERIES

The Standards Real Book (C, Bb or Eb)

A Beautiful Friendship	Days Of Wine And Roses	I Only Have Eyes For You	Old Folks	Summer Night
A Time For Love	Dreamsville	I'm A Fool To Want You	On A Clear Day	Summertime
Ain't No Sunshine	Easy To Love	Indian Summer	Our Love Is Here To Stay	Teach Me Tonight
Alice In Wonderland	Embraceable You	It Ain't Necessarily So	'Round Midnight	That Sunday, That Summer
All Of You	Falling In Love With Love	It Never Entered My Mind	Secret Love	The Girl From Ipanema
Alone Together	From This Moment On	It's You Or No One	September In The Rain	Then I'll Be Tired Of You
At Last	Give Me The Simple Life	Just One Of Those Things	Serenade In Blue	There's No You
Baltimore Oriole	Have You Met Miss Jones?	Love For Sale	Shiny Stockings	Time On My Hands
Bess, You Is My Woman	Hey There	Lover, Come Back To Me	Since I Fell For You	'Tis Autumn
Bluesette	I Can't Get Started	The Man I Love	So In Love	Where Or When
But Not For Me	I Concentrate On You	Mr. Lucky	So Nice (Summer Samba)	Who Cares?
Close Enough For Love	I Cover The Waterfront	My Funny Valentine	Some Other Time	With A Song In My Heart
Crazy He Calls Me	I Love You	My Heart Stood Still	Stormy Weather	You Go To My Head
Dancing In The Dark	I Loves You Porgy	My Man's Gone Now	The Summer Knows	**And Hundreds More!**

The New Real Book - Volume 1 (C, Bb or Eb)

Angel Eyes	Eighty One	I Thought About You	My Shining Hour	Shaker Song
Anthropology	E.S.P.	If I Were A Bell	Nature Boy	Skylark
Autumn Leaves	Everything Happens To Me	Imagination	Nefertiti	A Sleepin' Bee
Beautiful Love	Feel Like Makin' Love	The Island	Nothing Personal	Solar
Bernie's Tune	Footprints	Jersey Bounce	Oleo	Speak No Evil
Blue Bossa	Four	Joshua	Once I Loved	St. Thomas
Blue Daniel	Four On Six	Lady Bird	Out Of This World	Street Life
But Beautiful	Gee Baby Ain't I Good	Like Someone In Love	Pent Up House	Tenderly
Chain Of Fools	To You	Little Sunflower	Portrait Of Tracy	These Foolish Things
Chelsea Bridge	Gone With The Wind	Lush Life	Put It Where You Want It	This Masquerade
Compared To What	Here's That Rainy Day	Mercy, Mercy, Mercy	Robbin's Nest	Three Views Of A Secret
Darn That Dream	I Love Lucy	The Midnight Sun	Ruby, My Dear	Waltz For Debby
Desafinado	I Mean You	Monk's Mood	Satin Doll	Willow Weep For Me
Early Autumn	I Should Care	Moonlight In Vermont	Search For Peace	**And Many More!**

The New Real Book Play-Along CDs (For Volume 1)

CD #1 - Jazz Classics - Lady Bird, Bouncin' With Bud, Up Jumped Spring, Monk's Mood, Doors, Very Early, Eighty One, Voyage **& More!**

CD #2 - Choice Standards - Beautiful Love, Darn That Dream, Moonlight In Vermont, Trieste, My Shining Hour, I Should Care **& More!**

CD #3 - Pop-Fusion - Morning Dance, Nothing Personal, La Samba, Hideaway, This Masquerade, Three Views Of A Secret, Rio **& More!**

World-Class Rhythm Sections, featuring Mark Levine, Larry Dunlap, Sky Evergreen, Bob Magnusson, Keith Jones, Vince Lateano & Tom Hayashi

The New Real Book - Volume 2 (C, Bb or Eb)

Afro-Centric	Django	I'm Glad There Is You	Nica's Dream	Stablemates
After You've Gone	Equinox	Impressions	Once In A While	Stardust
Along Came Betty	Exactly Like You	In Your Own Sweet Way	Perdido	Sweet And Lovely
Bessie's Blues	Falling Grace	It's The Talk Of The Town	Rosetta	That's All
Black Coffee	Five Hundred Miles High	Jordu	Sea Journey	There Is No Greater Love
Blues For Alice	Freedom Jazz Dance	Killer Joe	Senor Blues	'Til There Was You
Body And Soul	Giant Steps	Lullaby Of The Leaves	September Song	Time Remembered
Bolivia	Harlem Nocturne	Manha De Carneval	Seven Steps To Heaven	Turn Out The Stars
The Boy Next Door	Hi-Fly	The Masquerade Is Over	Silver's Serenade	Unforgettable
Bye Bye Blackbird	Honeysuckle Rose	Memories Of You	So Many Stars	While We're Young
Cherokee	I Hadn't Anyone 'Til You	Moment's Notice	Some Other Blues	Whisper Not
A Child Is Born	I'll Be Around	Mood Indigo	Song For My Father	Will You Still Be Mine?
Cold Duck Time	I'll Get By	My Ship	Sophisticated Lady	You're Everything
Day By Day	Ill Wind	Naima	Spain	**And Many More!**

The New Real Book - Volume 3 (C, Bb, Eb or Bass clef)

Actual Proof	Dolphin Dance	I Hear A Rhapsody	Maiden Voyage	Speak Like A Child
Ain't That Peculiar	Don't Be That Way	If You Could See Me Now	Moon And Sand	Spring Is Here
Almost Like Being In Love	Don't Blame Me	In A Mellow Tone	Moonglow	Stairway To The Stars
Another Star	Emily	In A Sentimental Mood	My Girl	Star Eyes
Autumn Serenade	Everything I Have Is Yours	Inner Urge	On Green Dolphin Street	Stars Fell On Alabama
Bird Of Beauty	For All We Know	Invitation	Over The Rainbow	Stompin' At The Savoy
Black Nile	Freedomland	The Jitterbug Waltz	Prelude To A Kiss	Sweet Lorraine
Blue Moon	The Gentle Rain	Just Friends	Respect	Taking A Chance On Love
Butterfly	Get Ready	Just You, Just Me	Ruby	This Is New
Caravan	A Ghost Of A Chance	Knock On Wood	The Second Time Around	Too High
Ceora	Heat Wave	The Lamp Is Low	Serenata	(Used To Be A) Cha Cha
Close Your Eyes	How Sweet It Is	Laura	The Shadow Of Your Smile	When Lights Are Low
Creepin'	I Fall In Love Too Easily	Let's Stay Together	So Near, So Far	You Must Believe In Spring
Day Dream	I Got It Bad	Lonely Woman	Solitude	**And Many More!**

The All Jazz Real Book

Over 540 pages of tunes as recorded by: Miles, Trane, Bill Evans, Scofield, Cannonball, Brecker, Yellowjackets, Bird, Mulgrew Miller, Kenny Werner, MJQ, McCoy Tyner, Kurt Elling, Brad Mehldau, Don Grolnick, Kenny Garrett, Patitucci, Jerry Bergonzi, Stanley Clarke, Tom Harrell, Herbie Hancock, Horace Silver, Stan Getz, Sonny Rollins, and MORE!

Includes a free CD of many of the melodies (featuring Bob Sheppard & Friends.). $44 list price. Available in C, Bb, Eb

The European Real Book

An amazing collection of some of the greatest jazz compositions ever recorded! Available in C, Bb and Eb. $40

- Over 100 of Europe's best jazz writers.
- 100% accurate, composer-approved charts.
- 400 pages of fresh, exciting sounds from virtually every country in Europe.
- Sher Music's superior legibility and signature calligraphy makes reading the music easy.

Listen to FREE MP3 FILES of many of the songs at **www.shermusic.com!**

See **www.shermusic.com** for more information, including a complete list of tunes in all our fake books.

To order, call (800) 444-7437 or fax (707) 763-2038

SHER MUSIC JAZZ PUBLICATIONS

The Real Easy Book Vol. 1
TUNES FOR BEGINNING IMPROVISERS

Published by Sher Music Co. in conjunction with the Stanford Jazz Workshop. $22 list price.

The easiest tunes from Horace Silver, Eddie Harris, Freddie Hubbard, Red Garland, Sonny Rollins, Cedar Walton, Wes Montgomery Cannonball Adderly, etc. Get yourself or your beginning jazz combo sounding good right away with the first fake book ever designed for the beginning improviser.
Available in C, Bb, Eb and Bass Clef.

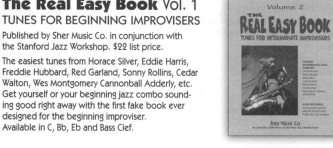

The Real Easy Book Vol. 2
TUNES FOR INTERMEDIATE IMPROVISERS

Published by Sher Music Co. in conjunction with the Stanford Jazz Workshop. Over 240 pages. $29.

The best intermediate-level tunes by: Charlie Parker, John Coltrane, Miles Davis, John Scofield, Sonny Rollins, Horace Silver, Wes Montgomery, Freddie Hubbard, Cal Tjader, Cannonball Adderly, and more!
Both volumes feature instructional material tailored for each tune. Perfect for jazz combos!
Available in C, Bb, Eb and Bass Clef.

The Real Easy Book Vol. 3
A SHORT HISTORY OF JAZZ

Published by Sher Music Co. in conjunction with the Stanford Jazz Workshop. Over 200 pages. $25.

History text and tunes from all eras and styles of jazz. Perfect for classroom use. Available in C, Bb, Eb and Bass Clef versions.

The Best of Sher Music Co. Real Books
100+ TUNES YOU NEED TO KNOW

A collection of the best-known songs from the world leader in jazz fake books – Sher Music Co.!
Includes songs by: Miles Davis, John Coltrane, Bill Evans, Duke Ellington, Antonio Carlos Jobim, Charlie Parker, John Scofield, Michael Brecker, Weather Report, Horace Silver, Freddie Hubbard, Thelonious Monk, Cannonball Adderley, and many more!
$26. Available in C, Bb, Eb and Bass Clef.

The Serious Jazz Book II
THE HARMONIC APPROACH

By Barry Finnerty, Endorsed by: Joe Lovano, Jamey Aebersold, Hubert Laws, Mark Levine, etc.

- A 200 page, exhaustive study of how to master the harmonic content of songs.
- Contains explanations of every possible type of chord that is used in jazz.
- Clear musical examples to help achieve real harmonic control over melodic improvisation.
- For any instrument. $32. Money back gurantee!

The Serious Jazz Practice Book By Barry Finnerty

A unique and comprehensive plan for mastering the basic building blocks of the jazz language. It takes the most widely-used scales and chords and gives you step-by-step exercises that dissect them into hundreds of cool, useable patterns.
Includes CD - $30 list price.

"The book I've been waiting for!" – Randy Brecker.

"The best book of intervallic studies I've ever seen."
– Mark Levine

The Jazz Theory Book

By Mark Levine, the most comprehensive Jazz Theory book ever published! $38 list price.
- Over 500 pages of text and over 750 musical examples.
- Written in the language of the working jazz musician, this book is easy to read and user-friendly. At the same time, it is the most comprehensive study of jazz harmony and theory ever published.
- Mark Levine has worked with Bobby Hutcherson, Cal Tjader, Joe Henderson, Woody Shaw, and many other jazz greats.

Jazz Piano Masterclass With Mark Levine
"THE DROP 2 BOOK"

The long-awaited book from the author of "The Jazz Piano Book!" A complete study on how to use "drop 2" chord voicings to create jazz piano magic! 68 pages, plus CD of Mark demonstrating each exercise. $19 list.

"Will make you sound like a real jazz piano player in no time." – Jamey Aebersold

Metaphors For The Musician
By Randy Halberstadt

This practical and enlightening book will help any jazz player or vocalist look at music with "new eyes." Designed for any level of player, on any instrument, "Metaphors For The Musician" provides numerous exercises throughout to help the reader turn these concepts into musical reality.

Guaranteed to help you improve your musicianship. 330 pages – $29 list price. Satisfaction guaranteed!

The Jazz Musicians Guide To Creative Practicing
By David Berkman

Finally a book to help musicians use their practice time wisely! Covers tune analysis, breaking hard tunes into easy components, how to swing better, tricks to playing fast bebop lines, and much more! 150+pages, plus CD. $29 list.

"Fun to read and bursting with things to do and ponder." – Bob Mintzer

The 'Real Easy' Ear Training Book
By Roberta Radley

For all musicians, regardless of instrument or experience, this is the most comprehensive book on "hearing the changes" ever published!
- Covers both beginning and intermediate ear training exercises.
- Music Teachers: You will find this book invaluable in teaching ear training to your students.

Book includes 168 pages of instructional text and musical examples, plus two CDs! $29 list price.

The Jazz Singer's Guidebook By David Berkman
A COURSE IN JAZZ HARMONY AND SCAT SINGING FOR THE SERIOUS JAZZ VOCALIST

A clear, step-by-step approach for serious singers who want to improve their grasp of jazz harmony and gain a deeper understanding of music fundamentals.

This book will change how you hear music and make you a better singer, as well as give you the tools to develop your singing in directions you may not have thought possible.

$26 – includes audio CD demonstrating many exercises.

LATIN MUSIC BOOKS, CDs, DVD

The Latin Real Book (C, Bb or Eb)

The only professional-level Latin fake book ever published!
Over 570 pages. Detailed transcriptions exactly as recorded by:

Ray Barretto	Arsenio Rodriguez	Manny Oquendo	Ivan Lins
Eddie Palmieri	Tito Rodriguez	Puerto Rico All-Stars	Djavan
Fania All-Stars	Orquesta Aragon	Issac Delgaldo	Tom Jobim
Tito Puente	Beny Moré	Ft. Apache Band	Toninho Horta
Ruben Blades	Cal Tjader	Dave Valentin	Joao Bosco
Los Van Van	Andy Narell	Paquito D'Rivera	Milton Nascimento
NG La Banda	Mario Bauza	Clare Fischer	Leila Pinheiro
Irakere	Dizzy Gilllespie	Chick Corea	Gal Costa
Celia Cruz	Mongo Santamaria	Sergio Mendes	**And Many More!**

The Latin Real Book Sampler CD

12 of the greatest Latin Real Book tunes as played by the original artists: Tito Puente, Ray Barretto, Andy Narell, Puerto Rico Allstars, Bacacoto, etc. $16 list price. Available in U.S.A. only.

The Conga Drummer's Guidebook By Michael Spiro

Includes CD - $28 list price. The only method book specifically designed for the intermediate to advanced conga drummer. It goes behind the superficial licks and explains how to approach any Afro-Latin rhythm with the right feel, so you can create a groove like the pros!.

"This book is awesome. Michael is completely knowledgable about his subject."
– Dave Garibaldi

"A breakthrough book for all students of the conga drum."
– Karl Perazzo

Introduction to the Conga Drum - DVD
By Michael Spiro

For beginners, or anyone needing a solid foundation in conga drum technique.

Jorge Alabe – "Mike Spiro is a great conga teacher. People can learn real conga technique from this DVD."

John Santos – "A great musician/teacher who's earned his stripes"

1 hour, 55 minutes running time. $25.

Muy Caliente!

Afro-Cuban Play-Along CD and Book
Rebeca Mauleón - Keyboard
Oscar Stagnaro - Bass
Orestes Vilató - Timbales
Carlos Caro - Bongos
Edgardo Cambon - Congas
Over 70 min. of smokin' Latin grooves!
Stereo separation so you can eliminate the bass or piano. Play-along with a rhythm section featuring some of the top Afro-Cuban musicians in the world! $18.

The True Cuban Bass

By Carlos Del Puerto, (bassist with Irakere) and **Silvio Vergara**, $22.

For acoustic or electric bass; English and Spanish text; Includes CDs of either historic Cuban recordings or Carlos playing each exercise; Many transcriptions of complete bass parts for tunes in different Cuban styles – the roots of Salsa.

101 Montunos
By Rebeca Mauleón

The only comprehensive study of Latin piano playing ever published.

- Bi-lingual text (English/Spanish)
- 2 CDs of the author demonstrating each montuno
- Covers over 100 years of Afro-Cuban styles, including the danzón, guaracha, mambo, merengue and songo—from Peruchin to Eddie Palmieri. $28

The Salsa Guide Book
By Rebeca Mauleón

The only complete method book on salsa ever published! 260 pages. $25.

Carlos Santana – "A true treasure of knowledge and information about Afro-Cuban music."
Mark Levine, author of The Jazz Piano Book. – "This is the book on salsa."
Sonny Bravo, pianist with Tito Puente – "This will be the salsa 'bible' for years to come."
Oscar Hernández, pianist with Rubén Blades – "An excellent and much needed resource."

The Brazilian Guitar Book
By Nelson Faria, one of Brazil's best new guitarists.

- Over 140 pages of comping patterns, transcriptions and chord melodies for samba, bossa, baião, etc.
- Complete chord voicings written out for each example.
- Comes with a CD of Nelson playing each example.
- The most complete Brazilian guitar method ever published! $28.

Joe Diorio – "Nelson Faria's book is a welcome addition to the guitar literature. I'm sure those who work with this volume wiill benefit greatly"

Inside The Brazilian Rhythm Section
By Nelson Faria and Cliff Korman

This is the first book/CD package ever published that provides an opportunity for bassists, guitarists, pianists and drummers to interact and play-along with a master Brazilian rhythm section. Perfect for practicing both accompanying and soloing.

$28 list price for book and 2 CDs - including the charts for the CD tracks and sample parts for each instrument, transcribed from the recording.

The Latin Bass Book
A PRACTICAL GUIDE
By Oscar Stagnaro

The only comprehensive book ever published on how to play bass in authentic Afro-Cuban, Brazilian, Caribbean, Latin Jazz & South American styles. $34.

Over 250 pages of transcriptions of Oscar Stagnaro playing each exercise. Learn from the best!

Includes: 3 Play-Along CDs to accompany each exercise, featuring world-class rhythm sections.

Afro-Caribbean Grooves for Drumset

By **Jean-Philippe Fanfant,** drummer with Andy narell's band, Sakesho.

Covers grooves from 10 Caribbean nations, arranged for drumset.

Endorsed by Peter Erskine, Horacio Hernandez, etc.

CD includes both audio and video files. $25.